BLESSED
ARE THE
STRESSED

BLESSED
ARE THE
STRESSED

Secrets to a Happy Heart
from a Crabby Mystic

Mary Lea Hill, FSP

auline
BOOKS & MEDIA
Boston

Library of Congress Cataloging-in-Publication Data

Hill, Mary Lea.
  Blessed are the stressed : secrets to a happy heart from a crabby mystic /
Mary Lea Hill, FSP.
      pages cm
  Includes bibliographical references.
  ISBN 978-0-8198-1229-2 (pbk.) -- ISBN 0-8198-1229-3 (pbk.)
  1. Beatitudes--Meditations. I. Title.
  BT382.H55 2016
  226.9'306--dc23

                        2015015614

Cover design by Rosana Usselmann

Cover photo: istockphoto.com/© wragg

Published by Pauline Books & Media, 50 Saint Pauls Avenue, Boston, MA 02130-3491

Printed in the U.S.A.

www.pauline.org

Pauline Books & Media is the publishing house of the Daughters of St. Paul, an international congregation of women religious serving the Church with the communications media.

1 2 3 4 5 6 7 8 9   20 19 18 17 16

In memory of my parents, Lee and Alvada,
and my brother and sister,
Lawrence and Marjorie,
who even now enjoy eternal happiness.

Contents

The Beatitudes
in Matthew 5:1–12 and Luke 6:20–26

The Sermon on the Mount Continues
in Matthew 5:13–7:29

Acknowledgments

The New Testament Scripture quotations used in this work are taken from *The New Testament: St. Paul Catholic Edition,* translated by Mark A. Wauck, copyright © 2000 by the Society of St. Paul, Staten Island, New York, and are used by permission. All rights reserved.

Most of the Scripture quotations from the book of Psalms are taken from *The Psalms: A Translation from the Hebrew,* edited by Miguel Miguens, copyright © 1997 by the Society of St. Paul, Staten Island, New York, and are used by permission. All rights reserved.

All other Old Testament Scripture quotations are taken from the *New Revised Standard Version Bible: Catholic Edition,* copyright © 1989, 1993, Division of Christian Education of the National Council of the Churches of Christ in the United States of America. Used by permission. All rights reserved.

The writings of Mother Teresa of Calcutta © by the Mother Teresa Center, exclusive licensee throughout the world of the Missionaries of Charity for the works of Mother Teresa. Used with permission.

Introduction ⨯⨯⨯⨯⨯⨯⨯⨯⨯⨯⨯⨯⨯⨯⨯⨯⨯⨯⨯⨯⨯⨯⨯⨯⨯⨯

The beatitudes are arguably the best known part of the Gospel. I suspect that they are, on that evidence alone, among the most important words in the New Testament. Because they are familiar to us, they easily roll off the tongue as we read them, almost as easily as the words of a well-known song repeated unconsciously. Generally it is said that familiarity breeds contempt, but I would say that with the beatitudes familiarity breeds comfort.

And so a question arises here: Is this sense of comfort a good or bad thing? Was comfort actually the motivation of Jesus when he proclaimed the beatitudes? A question also arises about the word *blessed* itself. What does it imply? Sometimes it is translated simply as *happy*. The secret to understanding the beatitudes lies in understanding these words.

As an introduction, let us just say that the difference between happiness and beatitude is easy to see in our culture. How many people do we know who are happy with how things are in their lives? How many are totally content with who they are and with what they have achieved, and wouldn't change a thing? They are happy as far as this world's happiness goes!

Our culture, however, tells us we are not happy and certainly not satisfied. We actually deserve more and better. Advertising has become the new asceticism, and it is dictating the parameters of our earthly paradise. These advertisers are, in fact, not wrong in prompting us toward more and better, because we are always in search of something beyond what we have. We know this *more* and this *better* to be the ultimate good, beauty, and truth whom we call God. Saint Augustine could offer his famous quotation as a good advertising slogan for eternal happiness: "Our hearts are restless, O Lord, until they rest in you."

Blessed Are the Stressed is not a scholarly treatment of the beatitudes; rather, it is a friendly stroll through them. We will stop to regard this aspect and that meaning in an attempt to get a better idea of how Jesus defines holiness. Together let us look at the beatitudes, savoring the words, mulling over the promises, but, most importantly, making them the hallmark of our lives.

The Beatitudes

When he saw the crowds he went up the mountain. After
he sat down his disciples came to him, and he opened
his mouth and taught them, saying,
"Blessed are the poor in spirit,
for theirs is the Kingdom of Heaven.
Blessed are those who mourn,
for they shall be comforted.
Blessed are the meek,
for they shall inherit the earth.
Blessed are those who hunger and thirst to do God's will,
for they shall have their fill.
Blessed are the merciful,
for they shall receive mercy.
Blessed are the pure of heart,
for they shall see God.
Blessed are the peacemakers,
for they shall be called sons of God.
Blessed are those who are persecuted for doing God's will,
for theirs is the Kingdom of Heaven.
Blessed are you when they insult you and persecute you
and say every sort of evil thing against you on account
of me; rejoice and be glad, because your reward will be
great in Heaven—they persecuted the prophets before
you in the same way." (Mt 5:1–12)

Then he raised his eyes to his disciples and said,
"Blessed are you poor,
    for yours is the Kingdom of God.
Blessed are you who hunger now,
    for you shall have your fill.
Blessed are you who weep now,
    for you shall laugh.
Blessed are you when men hate you and exclude you and
    insult you and reject your name as evil on account of
    the Son of Man; rejoice on that day and leap for joy—
    behold, your reward will be great in Heaven,
    because their fathers did the same to the prophets.
But woe to you rich,
    for you have your delights!
Woe to you who are full now,
    for you shall be hungry!
Woe, you who laugh now,
    for you shall mourn and wail!
Woe, when all men speak well of you,
for their fathers did the same to the false prophets!"
    (Lk 6:20–26)

"The beatitudes are the final crowning of the divine action in a soul. They are the efficacious means to attaining absolute happiness. They are an invitation to practice the virtues, even the most difficult ones."

—Blessed James Alberione[1]

4

Coming to Terms

Some concepts

We used to have a convent in a very interesting part of New York City—somewhere between dangerous and not-so-much. Ambitious would-be criminals occasionally hoisted themselves up the side of the building, seeking access through the roof; all manner of grates and bars kept us in, and guard dogs kept others out. So, it was hardly surprising when a visiting Italian sister, on her way out for the day, reported to the superior what she thought was a bomb at the front gate. Sister superior quickly mustered the troops. Several sisters jumped into gear and summoned New York's Finest, who came immediately with a full bomb squad. They briskly shepherded all the sisters to safety in the back yard. Moments later, from several big, burly cops came New York's finest laughter. They announced to the twittering flock of nuns that the threat was only a sleeping vagrant. When the original herald of the news came home was and told what happened, she just rolled her eyes and said in her distinctive accent,

"That's what I said: there's a *bom* out front!" She had probably hoped we would make him lunch; instead we made a scene!

Terms are interesting and important, but very often lead to confusion because they can so easily be misunderstood or misused. Before wading into the accounts of the beatitudes we need to check out a term. What exactly does *blessed* mean?

Our first time being blessed probably took place in this context: "*Achoo!*" "Bless you!"

We take this exchange for granted, but how did it begin? We are told that blessing the sneezer began during one of the influenza attacks of the past. It was hoped that the one who sneezed would not be headed to the sick bed. Now it's like an automatic reflex. Even if it's muttered mindlessly, I prefer it to alternative responses like "*Ewww!*" or "Just use your sleeve, will you?"

"God bless" is exactly what it says, while the less committed "Bless you" implies at least best wishes. Every attempt to live out one of the beatitudes invokes God's care and kindness. God's special grace lands on us. What could be better? That's top-tier!

> *. . . Respond with blessings, for this is your calling and in this way you will obtain a blessing. (1 Pt 3:9)*

And you

Are you in the habit of freely bestowing blessings? What about being a blessing to someone?

Whoa Is Me!

Luke's Version

Horses are so beautiful and powerful! It is always a thrill to see them running wild and free across sunlit hillsides, manes and tails flying. Of course, horses are very big animals. I used to dream of riding. I have a photo from the good old days of pre-school me looking petrified sitting atop a rather short horse, with Dad protectively alongside. I don't remember this first ride, but I shudder at the thought of my second meeting with a member of that species at a county fair. The only problem for me was having to actually stay on top of the noble steed. I clambered up one side and promptly slid off the other. Even the horse looked back at me with disdain. I've sworn off riding since that day. Years later at the Grand Canyon, a guide suggested that we travel down the side trails on horseback. It was tempting until I glanced across at the riders coming down one narrow, rocky trail. The horses delicately sashayed along, swinging their riders way over the edge of the trail. *No thanks,* I thought. *I don't want a constant bird's-eye view of where I'll end up if I slip off this time.*

I'm certain had I ever made it to ride atop a horse, even at a steady clop, the first thing out of my mouth would have been, "Whoa, Nelly, or whoever you are!" Yes, I'm skittish, but also cautious.

This is how it is with half of the beatitudes as Luke recalls them. Midway in the account, he switches from *blessed* to *woe.* These woes serve to stop us in our tracks like a big old "Whoa!" *Hold up a minute and consider this. Danger ahead, watch your step. Woe* is a note of warning. It's as if, in this version of the beatitudes, Jesus is saying, "Whoa to you rich, for you have your delights! Whoa to you who are full now . . . , whoa, you who laugh now . . . , whoa when all speak well of you. . . ."

If only my people would listen to me,
if only Israel would live up to my ways,
in an instant would I subdue their enemies
and extend my hands against their oppressors.
(Ps 81:14–15)

And you

Looking at your own way of discipleship, can you imagine the Lord whispering a "Whoa!" to you? Pray about it.

Taffy Pull

Fault

Let's have our little talk on sin right up front and get it over with.

Most of us are familiar with the seven capital sins—principal sins of human nature, the underside of our natural goodness, that is: pride, greed, envy, lust, anger, gluttony, and sloth. These are expressions not of our nature as God planned it, but of rebellion, distrust, disbelief, jealousy, and so on— the inheritance of original sin. Generally one of the sins predominates, hence "our predominant fault." We speak of "faults" and not of "predominant sins" because, until activated, they are only tendencies or inclinations.

Suppose one's predominant fault is greed. I'm always in need. Although I have enough of everything and need nothing, I want something else: I don't just admire or appreciate it, but I want it and I *will* get it.

Let me share a rather innocent example. When I was in the first grade, my mother sent me on an errand. I came back with a bag of salt water taffy. I admired it all the way home and set my heart on the chocolate one. My mother wisely put the bag in a jar on the bookcase. "After supper," she promised. Meanwhile, my sister spied the jar and helped herself. After supper I found my anticipated treasure gone. Oh, the early-onset angst! My little self reprimanded my honesty, obedience, and lack of alertness. Why didn't I remove that piece on the way home? Why did my sister have to take the very piece I wanted? Of course, the better me knew the bag of candy was for the whole family; I should generously offer the others first dibs.

You may be thinking: "Relax. You were just a little girl." True, but I was a little girl who spent a lot of time mulling over "good, better, best," *and* bad.

The pull of the capital sins is constant in life, but Jesus has given us a game plan for overriding these tendencies: the beatitudes.

Incline my heart to your testimonies
rather than toward selfish gain.
Restrain my heart from giving attention to empty things;
let me live in your way. (Ps 119:36–37)

And you

As an adult you will find you desire many things from life: good, better, best, *and* bad. How do you stir yourself toward the way of Christian discipleship? Which beatitude do you find most helpful?

Tips

Happiness

As far as happiness goes, the beatitudes seem unrealistic, exaggerated, and obscure. Although we usually set them aside as a poetic manifesto of the Messiah, we are about to venture into them on a quest for meaning. And when we say we seek meaning, we really ask for relevance. What are these statements to you and me?

We know the Gospel is not just an historical document to be read as the heritage of Christians. No, the Gospel is the living Word of God—it speaks to us today. Ideally, it will be a conversation between Jesus and us.

There are four Gospels—four distinct accounts of the life and teachings of Jesus Christ—written at different times, in different places, for different audiences, with different emphases. We should totally get this if we watch weekend sporting events where questionable calls are reviewed from several angles on instant replay. In the Gospel accounts of

11

Matthew and Luke we can see the eight beatitudes from different angles.

The beatitudes are a central part of the great spiritual quest we are on in this life. You may recall the quest of Ulysses, the famous Greek hero who went off to war but found himself on an extended journey as he tried to return home to his wife and family. His quest seems quite exaggerated, whereas ours, though not as harrowing, is no less heroic. Jesus offers us the eight beatitudes as tips to measure our Christian heroics. The quest for Christian holiness laid out in the beatitudes has no ceiling, no upper limit. For example, has anyone ever been too poor in spirit, too meek, or too pure of heart? And neither does God run a one-size-fits-all establishment; he is the Master tailor. Clothe yourselves with Christ, advises Saint Paul. To do this we need to become familiar with the beatitudes, trying them on so we can better see what we look like in Christ.

> *Through faith you are all sons of God in Christ Jesus, for all of you who were baptized into Christ have clothed yourselves with Christ. (Gal 3:27)*

And you

Read over the two accounts of the beatitudes (see pp. 3–4). Try them on one by one. How do you "look" in them? Can you see how they will help you on your great quest?

The Pursuit

Happiness

The idea of pursuit has been an ever-popular theme in literature. In Francis Thompson's classic poem, *The Hound of Heaven*, God constantly pursues the soul. Today the theme often translates to the world of cinema. Modern filmmakers find endless delight in action-packed chase scenes, and often the film's ending seems anticlimactic because the whole premise was the pursuit.

The United States is built on this same premise. The *Declaration of Independence* clearly states that our God-given rights include the pursuit of happiness. We could say that this is the aim of the beatitudes as well: the pursuit of eternal happiness. Scholars contend that the Greek word for beatitude —*makários*—cannot be rendered as happiness. Technically that might be true, because *makários* means to be fully satisfied in eternal blessedness, whereas, according to the dictionary definition, happiness is a temporal satisfaction due to favorable circumstances. Basically, we are dealing with a word dispute. The Founders didn't tempt King George's wrath in order to chance favorable circumstances. They meant to break off from his constraints and create for themselves a life not necessarily easy, but one where they could freely pursue contentment. In our day, we seek abiding happiness generally found in a lifetime pursuit of our goals, culminating in a secure retirement. As Christians, this is identical to what the beatitudes mean in our spiritual quest for heaven. The beatitudes are attitudes refined over a lifetime, culminating in an eternal enjoyment of perfect happiness.

> *If you have been raised with Christ, seek the things that are above, where Christ is seated at God's right hand; think about the things that are above, not about things on earth, for you have died and your life is hidden with Christ in God. (Col 3:1–3)*

And you

Mother, the flag, and apple pie are down-home symbols of *life, liberty, and the pursuit of happiness*, don't you think? We proudly proclaim these values as our inalienable rights. Are they also bedrock values of your personal journey? Being respected, honored, and protected because of who you are; being free and responsible for your own thoughts and decisions; being able to pursue those desires and dreams that give you joy and fulfillment—what's not to love about that? These inalienable rights are also your unavoidable duties as citizens of God's Kingdom. How is your dual citizenship coming along?

What Are Beatitudes For?

Happiness

When do we begin our natural obsession about our looks? Young children are fascinated with mirrors and delighted with photos of themselves, but they're just curious. Grown-ups, instead, are quite concerned about the image they present to others. Just sit for an hour or two in the Los Angeles airport if you don't believe me. A lot of folks passing through give the impression that they're being followed by movie cameras. *Hope I'm coming across well. Got to give them my best!*

When it comes to best image, there must be millions of images of Christ, representing everyone's idea of his perfect manhood. For centuries artists have attempted to portray the Lord, from sketches in the catacombs, icons from the East, classic works from the likes of El Greco and Caravaggio, right up to the work of today's graffiti artists.

Personally, I would eliminate those masters who give Jesus an effeminate look. Jesus was a Mideastern Jew, so I expect he had a darker complexion and hair. His eyes would have been dark and lively, his smile quick and manly, his build that of a man used to manual labor. That's just my expectation, but we really don't know what Jesus looked like. Not even the Shroud of Turin, said to bear the impression of his dead body, gives us a good image. That we have no authentic depiction is a wise move on God's part, for without an actual image of Jesus, we can envision him as we like.

God himself did leave us an important impression of his Son, however, and it is found in the two Gospel accounts of the beatitudes. In Matthew 5 and Luke 6, Jesus offers us his self-portrait. His image is found in the beatitudes. To share in his mission, his hearers would have to become like him. The beatitudes are not exactly a "to-do list" but attitudes or ways of carrying out discipleship. Love, of course, is the goal of discipleship, but the beatitudes are what discipleship "looks" like.

"All will know by this that you are my disciples,
If you have love for one another." (Jn 13:35)

And you

Spend some time reading the beatitudes. Ask yourself: What did Jesus intend for me in speaking these words? Am I convinced that true beauty lies in the beatitudes?

Beauty-tudes

Definition

To bring the idea of beatitude into our present world, let's call it happiness. Technically it isn't the correct definition, but we have so little experience with beatitude that it's really not a household term. Even the happiness we know is often only the hope of happiness.

Happiness is not perfect here, but we try to trick ourselves into thinking it is hidden within some other *thing* like money, influence, power, beauty, relationships, agility, or freedom. Eventually these things prove imperfect because they fade and fail us.

We can have a certain portion of happiness now, but only as a gift, not as a possession or an accomplishment. When that sense of happiness deeply touches the soul, it becomes a taste of eternal beatitude.

What do we say about this idea of beatitude? What does the word even mean? Some authors, in the hope of popularizing the concept, have called it *attitude*, the "be-attitude."

Well, we do need a certain attitude in order to understand the meaning of the beatitudes. Perhaps we picture the state of beatitude as a cushion of clouds or an ethereal mist. Some sort of mystical music plays in the background and we feel calm. The idea of being lulled might appeal for a few moments, but life is the place for activity, for doing and achieving. How does eternal beatitude fit into that?

Is it then simply an obtuse word used to describe a totally unknown spiritual concept? We believe in heaven, but that's about as far as the mind can go: we assent to the unknown. Jessica Powers, in her poem "Heaven," describes eternal happiness simply as "something happening in the soul."[1] So what is beatitude in the here-and-now?

> *Although you haven't seen him you love him, and although you don't see him now you believe in him and rejoice with an inexpressible and glorious joy because you are attaining the salvation of your souls, the goal of your faith. (1 Pet 1:8–9)*

And you

Think of beatitude as a form of the word "beauty." Does beauty make you think of pleasure and perfection? We define God as eternal Beauty, Truth, and Goodness. Would you say then that the beatitudes are attitudes of eternal beauty?

The Eternal Award

Happiness

Are you a fan of award shows? Whether it's the Grammys, Oscars, Golden Globes, or SAGs, true fans breathlessly await the list of nominees. They spend time in useless speculation, constantly check Web sites, and purchase magazines. Ah, the glory of gossip, talk shows, and sightings! At last the evening arrives; we turn on our screens, lower the lights, strategically place snacks. We, the adoring public, are transfixed. "And the winner is. . . ." *"You've got to be KIDDING! No way!"*

When we are gathered for the grand, eternal awards show in heaven, will we be surprised as certain names are called? We expect the likes of our Lady, Saint Joseph, Saint Thérèse, or Saint Paul to be singled out. If the winners are all "big-name saints" we won't think twice, but what about the little, insignificant unknowns?

"Really, the man down the street, not Saint Francis of Assisi, is named *poorest*?"

"My second cousin, Molly, was the meekest?"

"That guy in politics really worked harder at justice than anyone else?"

"You're kidding: a superstar athlete wins for pure of heart?"

"Wow! Who knew these folks were so into this stuff?"

Suppose now, just suppose, your own name were called for one of these awards. What award would it be? Most merciful? Or the most Christ-like heart, in tune with the sorrows and sufferings of this world? Or the most aligned with God's will? Or, better yet, how about peacemaker par excellence? Can you imagine yourself winning one of these? If not, how about as runner-up? At least as one of the nominees? Even just under consideration? Well then, let's review the categories again, shall we?

> *"Behold, I am coming soon, and I will bring my rewards with me, to repay everyone according to their deeds. I am the Alpha and the Omega, the first and the last, the beginning and the end." (Rev 22:12–13)*

And you

Whether you place bets or not, everyone loves a winner. The qualities that guarantee success are subjective according to the contest, and victory is often relative. However, in the very real and all-important game of life, we play with accessible rules and high stakes. Are you a serious contender?

Doing Poorly

Poor in spirit

Perhaps our poverty is that we aren't poor. We may lack the very condition that will make us blessed and worthy of heaven according to the first beatitude. "But, I am kind of poor," you say. "Look at all the bills I have, and my credit cards are maxed out. I'm definitely poor!" Not really, at least not by the world's standards, where millions of people live (and often die) hand-to-mouth. Major necessities such as food and water are simply not always available. And, no, you aren't even poor by first-world standards. You have a roof over your head, even if it leaks; you have food, water, heat, *and bills.* The desperately poor don't have bills because they don't have any place to receive mail. They have no purchasing power at all. Furthermore, you have credit cards, and you had credit to max out. Many people will never be offered a credit card because they have no hope of ever being able to pay on credit. So, at best you can only claim to be on the upper crust of poverty.

The Kingdom of God is certainly in your sights, but don't confuse seeing and seizing. This is why Matthew added "in spirit" to his "blessed are the poor." These two little words indicate how we are practicing poverty—a distinguishing factor similar to someone saying aloud, "I love you," and adding under their breath, "in theory only." When we say we're poor in spirit, we're saying that we really "get it." Poverty isn't having or not having; it's using properly whatever you have. Poverty of spirit is a heart condition: in my heart I'm detached from everything and I'm centered on God. I want God and I will use everything else as a means to be with him. What does that entail? I'm not lamenting what I lack, nor am I reveling in what I have. *I* am living life, using and sharing who I am and what I have.

"For the spirit is willing,
but the flesh is weak." (Mt 26:41)

And you

In spirit is how you go about living. It is the spunk, the verve, the attention, and the nerve with which you empty yourself of all that does not lead to the Kingdom of God. Are you a spirited believer?

Poverty Is Like Fishing

Poor in spirit

What a marvelous find! My sister and I quickly filled a paper sack with the fish we found lying on the banks of the pond. Since we were on our way to church, we hid the bag in some bushes. When we triumphantly presented the find to our mother later that morning, she was—how shall I put it?—impressed. While I don't remember her exact words, she told us with a certain urgency to bring the fish back to where we found them. Being city girls, we hadn't a clue about quality control for fish, and they were very smelly, as I recall.

"Give a man a fish and you feed him for a day; teach him how to fish and you feed him for a lifetime," so the saying goes. This is where the virtue of poverty is like fishing. We often think of poverty as a negative practice: we're deprived, or we give up, or we do without. However, poverty is also, and above all, something positive. Blessed James Alberione taught his sons and daughters of the Pauline Family that their practice of poverty must renounce, produce, preserve, provide, and build. I'm not sure what is more challenging: to be born poor or to choose poverty. Father Alberione was speaking to those who choose to live poverty as religious, but his approach is appropriate to the beatitude in general. By *renouncing* what we could acquire, we keep our spirit trim and fit for the Kingdom. By *producing* we're exercising our creativity, finding ways to contribute to the good of all. By *preserving* we're maintaining what we do have, making it last longer, and respecting the gifts we've been given. By *providing* we're on the lookout for ways to care for ourselves, our works, and the needs of others. By *building* we're placing our energies and initiatives, our labor, and our love atop what has been done before so that God's work will be more visible to the world.

Jesus said to them, "Children, do you have any fish?" They answered him, "No." Then he said to them, "Cast the net to the right side of the boat and you'll find some." (Jn 21:5–6)

And you

Mull over how the positive aspects of poverty can influence your life. Will you suffer poverty, endure poverty, or flourish in the company of the poor Christ?

Abandon

Poor in spirit

More than giving up all one's possessions for love of God, poverty of spirit involves giving one's whole self to God. In other words, it means being empty of our own plans, desires, needs, and intentions. This is what is meant by *holy abandon* when we pray, "I am all yours and all that I possess I offer to you, my loving Jesus."

If you think this kind of spiritual availability belongs to a more romantic era, consider the case of the Englishman, John Randal Bradburne (1921–1979). After some years of military service, John converted to Catholicism and made several unsuccessful attempts to enter a monastery. Unsettled, he traveled to present-day Zimbabwe in search of a hermitage and became a Franciscan tertiary. After visiting a leper colony, he decided to stay as their caretaker. He bathed and bandaged the sores of the eighty lepers, cared for their huts, fed them, supplied for their needs, taught them songs, accompanied them as they died, and tended their graves. For

John this was happiness. Unfortunately, even this commitment came to an early end. After three years the Leprosy Association asked John to leave the colony because they thought that he was pampering the patients. Among other things he demanded that they be given proper food and not be made to wear ID numbers.

John secretly continued his ministrations by night. One evening a group from a rebel faction kidnapped and killed John. In life he had surrendered everything. He practiced a poverty of concern, of intent, of will, of desire. He found his security in total abandonment to God's will. And God rewarded John by fulfilling the three desires he had in life: to serve among lepers, die a martyr, and be buried in the Franciscan habit.

"Foxes have holes,
and the birds of the sky have nests,
but the Son of Man has nowhere to lay his head." (Lk 9:58)

And you

Total abandonment may not be for you. However, do you feel you could lay aside some of your plans to offer a service in Christ's name? Perhaps you could express poverty of spirit in some way—for example, to abandon the pleasure of smoking and use that money to serve those in need. You could also join a service group that will require an offering of time and energy.

Don't Cry Foul

Poor in spirit

When you go to a baseball game and have been lucky enough to secure a seat in the section that sees the most foul balls, you aren't going to sit there with a beer in one hand and a hotdog in the other. No, you're there at the ready with your glove securely on one hand and maybe some concession special in the other. If a foul ball heads your way, popcorn, peanuts, hotdog, and beer are as good as lost. Capturing the prize trumps everything!

Giving up stuff is not the heart of poverty of spirit; it's only a start. It might soften our grip on what seems so important, however. One needn't even give up anything for this type of poorness. Rich folks can also—and simultaneously—be poor of spirit. How so?

If we were to ask Epicurus, the ancient Greek philosopher, his reply would be: "To make a man happy, don't add to his riches but take from his desires." He also said: "It isn't possessions that make one rich, but the dignity with which one can do without."

Don't we all feel a kind of envy or awe of a person who had, if not "it all," at least a good portion of everything and who willingly gave it up or set it aside to give themselves to some need or cause? It amazes me that such souls exist, souls who can live on goodness alone. Many of us do all right with little, but given the opportunity we would gladly acquire more.

> *Have the same outlook among you that Christ Jesus had,*
> *who, though he was in the form of God,*
> *did not consider equality with God something to hold*
> *on to. (Phil 2:5–6)*

And you

Suppose for a moment that you won the lottery. You now have so much money that you can hardly think straight. Knowing yourself, what would be your first inclination? Reread the thoughts from Epicurus just above. Can you imagine something you would not seek with your new fortune? Even now in your modest situation, is there something you can purposefully do without and not feel you are forfeiting your dignity?

Selfies

Poor in spirit

As I write this book, selfies are the latest craze. Folks are turning their cameras on themselves in groups, in closets, before monuments, dangling over precipices, everywhere. And no one is safe from being corralled into *my* selfie. At least these overtly egotistical shots are eliminating the impulse to carve "Guess who was here" signs on every interesting landmark. I've been taking partial selfies for years: of my hand on the desk, of my foot on the floor, or of something so grandly out-of-focus it could have been anything at all. I'm hoping my accidental frames will contribute to my humility at least.

The beatitudes are our spiritual selfies. They are individual snapshots of our soul at work. As the world goes about its daily rounds, we spontaneously turn the camera inward to record the activity of grace.

We recognize how each beatitude is applicable in the here-and-now, as well as its promised spiritual meaning. The poor, those mourning, and the meek may in a certain sense have no boot straps with which to pull themselves up. Certainly God will provide for those who have no choice other than these states. Is the God we so fondly address as Father going to forget all these people from the beginning of time simply because they weren't spiritually in-the-know? Think of how many people today have no knowledge of Christianity or, for that matter, of any other organized religion. What did God say to Jonah about the people—God's people—of the pagan city of Nineveh, who didn't know their left hand from their right hand? He had pity on them because they were clueless. Natural human goodness enters in here— the sincerity of human virtue. Such folks would fail a catechism exam, but they have a natural goodness of spirit. They possess poverty of spirit: no conniving, grasping, hating, fighting.

> *As servants of God we commend ourselves in every way possible with great steadfastness . . . as poor yet enriching many, as having nothing yet possessing everything. (2 Cor 6:4,10)*

And you

Looking back at ourselves, we recognize how important poverty of spirit is, even as we make efforts to practice all the beatitudes. Learn to see yourself as an empty vessel available to be filled with meekness, righteousness, purity, mercy, sorrowfulness, peacefulness, and a sense of sacrifice.

Unrepeatable

Poor in spirit

In our world today the crime of identity theft has exploded. No one's personal information is secure. Our privacy and individuality don't seem to matter.

But identity is everything, because God made each of us an unrepeatable individual. Yet, almost unknowingly, some of us are ID thieves. Not that we are on the Web surfing for unsecured personal information, but we may have assumed someone else's identity nonetheless. It could be that we pretend to be someone we admire, perhaps a film star or just a very popular friend.

This is why youth is often a time of insecurity. It's a time of self-questioning and discovery. Who am I? Who is my family? Am I the same as my parents? Am I who my peers want me to be? Can I be someone now and someone else later on? Think of job changes, marriage breakups, remarriages and realignment of relatives, debilitating illness or injury, financial calamity or gain, etc. How do these affect how I know myself?

Enter authenticity!

Generally, we wouldn't buy unlabeled goods at the grocery store, simply because we don't know what the can or box contains. A few years back our community received some unlabeled cans. The cook, new in this country, prepared supper. From down the hallway we knew the evening's entrée was cat food, one of those little odiferous cans of mystery meat or fish. A lot of explaining, complaining, and refusal to eat ensued. No label leads to trouble.

And so we need authenticity. Labels help us identify the contents of food packaging. For people, authenticity lies in recognizing and accepting ourselves with all of our peculiarities, gifts, abilities, and attributes. This recognition and acceptance require a poverty of spirit. We look at ourselves in the mirror of our own spirit and find there the individual whom God loved into existence.

Jesus said to them, "Amen, amen, I say to you, before Abraham came to be, I am." (Jn 8:58)

And you

Who you really are is very important to God. Of course, you have to refine your virtues and address your weak points, but are you satisfied with your identity? Do you feel authentic? Can you look at yourself in a mirror and declare: "I am the loved and lovable son/daughter of God"?

15

"I'm Not a Mourning Person"

Mourn

The world has many types of people. Some are self-declared night owls. Some are comatose until their second cup of coffee. Others are proverbial "early birds." Then there are the happy, the melancholic, the angry, the aloof, the disinterested, the mothering, and the smothering. Some folks are equipped for any emergency, while others faint at the sight of blood. Some laugh easily, some appear quite somber. Our personalities come in many shapes and sizes. One area of life, however, can trip up all our social graces. That stumbling block is death. What do we do with death? We can't fix it, but neither can we ignore it. Death happens. It will happen to those we love—and it will happen to us.

Our own reactions to death can be surprising. "I am at a complete loss with death and with mourning. I'm simply not a mourning person," some say. Then you may be the perfect mourner. Jesus declares that mourning contains a blessing. He also says those who mourn will be comforted. In some cultures certain persons are called in for funerals—they are literally professional mourners. These people are always available, they possess the proper attire, and they know the chants, songs, or cadences of the customary sounds of mourning. You, instead, with all of your timidity and inadequacy can be the best mourner because you respect the pain of those who have lost a loved one, you inhabit the natural fear of the unknown, you have nothing to offer but your presence.

> *So when Jesus saw her [Mary] weeping, and the Jews who had come with her weeping . . . Jesus began to weep. (Jn 11:33–35)*

And you

In the Gospel account Jesus raises Lazarus from the dead and restores him to his sisters, Mary and Martha. As God, Jesus could do this. As humans we cannot, but we can join Jesus in his human reaction: he wept. Are you able to offer the comfort of your presence to those who mourn? *Blessed are those who mourn.*

Mourning Star

Mourn

Some years back I went through a bit of mourning. It involved a transfer: the loss of one of my favorite people. Who was it? Well, it was little old me. To myself I was lamenting: "I'm going to miss me when I'm gone." I was really going to miss what was so familiar and customary in my life at that point. I wasn't going to do "new" well; I was sure of it.

Thinking back on this, I realize that life is always new. Newness is almost a definition of life: every moment is new. Keeping this idea in mind helps us go through life's little mournings with flying colors.

What do we have to mourn? Well, one thing is lost opportunity. Some things are our own fault, as much as we prefer to simply label them mistakes. The fact is we did something bad or didn't do something good, and we deserve to allow ourselves a little honest regret. Sin or fault, it's not the end of the world. A little bit of regret is healthy. Life is a lot easier if we can stare at our own imperfection and smile. God loves the person he sees there. Isn't it freeing to be loved by someone who loves us just as we are? Someone not always remarking on our weight, our hair, our sense of humor, the way we walk or talk, except to affirm us. This is how God sees us. He only wants our good, and not only wants it but gives it to us. He also gives us *his own good,* which we know as grace. He's always more concerned to assist us to reach the best, to realize all the good we're capable of, and he fills whatever is lacking with his own goodness.

The benefit of regret is humility, in other words, being honest with ourselves and before our greatest admirer, God.

*"And bring the fatted calf—slaughter it and let's eat
         and celebrate—
this son of mine was dead,
     and has come back to life,
he was lost,
     and has been found." (Lk 15:23–24)*

And you

God is the loving father whose will is a warm embrace. He always offers us what is best and is always ready to welcome back the wanderer. Can you turn around and return to his plans when you realize you're pursuing a mistaken route?

Motherhood

Mourn

One day I was talking to a woman *of means*, as we discreetly describe the wealthy of our world, when her little boy did a nose-dive off his tricycle. Luckily, he landed on some manicured turf, not the rocky driveway. But he scrambled up, crying inconsolably, and raced right past his waiting mother into his nanny's arms. This is not meant as a judgment on nanny-hood or a statement on motherhood, but just an observation on the natural need to be comforted.

As Catholics we have a corner on comfort. Jesus built it into his family of faith. He gave us Mary, his own beloved Mother, to be our Mother. And he gave her to us at the very moment when he most needed her himself, as he hung in agony on the cross. Looking down on Mary and the Apostle John, Jesus said, "Behold your mother" (Jn 19:25). Ever since, whenever we have the least distress here in this valley of tears, we invoke Mary. In fact, we pray in Saint Bernard's *Memorare*, "I fly to you, O Virgin of Virgins, my Mother."

When we hurt and have been hurtful; when we have sinned and are sorrowful; when it's all just too much and we simply need some comfort, we find the love and consolation of our God in the arms of Mary.

According to the Litany of Loreto, Mary is the Comforter of the Afflicted, a very motherly title. So also, when our sorrow is the deep kind brought on by mourning, we turn to Mary. In fact, we learn about life best from our mothers, and Mary is the one who best modeled mourning for us. One of the most inspiring pieces of art in the Christian world is Michelangelo's *Pietà,* in which Mary is depicted in dignified devastation and holy hope as she cradles her Son's dead body. Let's always go to her in all our sorrows and our joys. When God created mothers, he saw how good it was for us. May we let our gratitude show.

His mother kept all these things in her heart. . . . (Lk 2:51)

And you

Mourning is part of everyone's life. We all lose loved ones, but we also lose parts of our life that we hold dear. Have you learned to bring your sorrows to Mary for her advice and consolation? What has she taught you about mourning?

For What Else Shall We Mourn?

Mourn

When we mourn, whether it's with someone suffering a loss or because of some situation we've heard about that weighs on our hearts, we have to admit that we, too, are suffering. In 1963, during his speech at the infamous wall dividing the city of Berlin, President John F. Kennedy made the history-changing statement: *"Ich bin ein Berliner!"* ("I am a Berliner!"). By uttering these words within earshot of the East Berlin government, and by their broadcast within earshot of the entire world, the President consciously joined himself to the struggle of the citizens of that city.

The *Imitation of Christ* says: "The Lord frequently visits the heart of man" (Book II, Chapter 1). God makes these little forays into our hearts to help us feel some of what he feels for the needs and sorrows of the world. It is so easy to close ourselves up within our securities when others desperately need our prayerful support. "Steel your heart," we sometimes hear it said. While we want to be strong people, we don't want hearts that are literally made of steel. We want to be pliable, easily subject to a whole gamut of human emotion. "If anyone is weak, I too am weak!" says Saint Paul. "If anyone is led into sin, I too am ablaze with indignation!" (2 Cor 11:29). Because in Christ we are one body—one Mystical Body, but still *one* body—we should feel with one another. Who has to flee from their homeland, who is threatened with certain death if they don't reject their faith, who is wrongly imprisoned, and we are not drawn into that suffering? This is the blessing of a sensitive heart that can mourn the presence of sin and its consequences.

> *"How often I wished*
> *to gather your children,*
> *the way a hen gathers her brood*
> *under her wings,*
> *but you would not!" (Mt 23:37)*

And you

How often do we enter into the anguish of the fictitious characters of our favorite TV dramas and yet are ambivalent about the struggles of folks living in our own neighborhood. In her book, *Hymns to the Church*, Gertrud von Le Fort has the Church say this consoling line, "For the sorrow of the world has become blessed, because it has been loved."[1] Yes, Christ loved the world's sorrows into blessings. Will you join him?

Let Them Eat Cake

Mourn

Mourning is very often a painful prospect, like salt in a wound, yet sometimes it's a cleansing pain. It may be that we're mourning some past transgression of our own— perhaps a lie that changed a relationship, some dishonest gain that can't be rectified, or some harsh words that caused us to lose contact with a friend. "A sobering knowledge also comes to the person who now mourns for past error. This mourning is not a depression or lament. Rather the mourning is a type of seasoning, a solemn yet earnest dedication," says J. Brian Bransfield.[1]

We've already chastised ourselves for whatever these sins were. We've even confessed them, but sacramental absolution doesn't necessarily cancel our regret; if anything, it should strengthen our resolve, our "earnest dedication," to react differently from now on.

Not all of us have to face the total destruction of all we hold dear, nor come to our end on the guillotine as did Marie

Antoinette, the Queen of France at the time of the French Revolution (1789–1799). She is often quoted as saying, "Let them eat cake!" when told that the citizens of Paris were starving for bread. Historians don't put much stock in these words, but all agree that her lifestyle made her appear heartless. In her last days of freedom, it seems Marie Antoinette tried to help the peasants at her country estate, but it was too little too late.

A lot of regret can be avoided by being attentive and involved in the world around us.

We should let our hearts feel penitent, that is, always ready to apologize to God and others for our faults and failings and those we see around us. To mourn includes marking off, as it were, the evil that happens in the world from the good that was given by God. When he created our world, God seasoned it with his blessing; he pronounced it "good." Let us offer a blessing when we see God's goodness marred by human thoughtlessness—of others or our own.

For grief which is directed toward God produces a repentance that leads to salvation and is not to be regretted, whereas sorrow in a purely human sense brings death. (2 Cor 7:10)

And you

Do you understand the beatitude that promises comfort if we mourn? Do you agree that mourning our regrets is a healthy and holy thing?

20

Sick and Tired

Mourn

We like life to be neat, tidy, and predictable. When the pressure is on, everything is topsy-turvy. Perhaps we are sick and feel tired. In fact, we are sick and tired of being sick and tired!

Someone will always try to buoy us up with cheery thoughts. "All will be well," they say. Some realists chime in with words of resignation and a stale sense of peace. A Greek philosopher named Heraclitus once noted that it's not good to have everything go as we desire, for we can't value health without sickness, good without evil, satisfaction without hunger, nor rest without weariness.

Being sick and tired, literally or not, may be a learning experience. It is good to identify what is causing this lethargy. "I've gone through all the things behind this down-and-out feeling," you say. "My job, my health, my mortgage, my securities, my marriage, my future—it's all giving me high blood pressure and ulcers. Basically, I'm a wreck. I feel like the dreams of my youth have died and taken me with them. I'm kind of mourning, I guess."

If this be the case, in the spirit of Heraclitus we should ask ourselves what we can learn through this kind of mourning. Mourning gives vent to remorse and sorrow, and we can certainly feel these when we think of the state of our life. But true mourning should have at least a cast of hope, and with hope a certain peace. In moments like these we should turn to our Great Consoler—the one who knows the mysteries of life and death. At that point our mourning becomes a prayer.

Why, my soul, are you depressed and moan within me?
Hope in the LORD that I will praise him still,
the salvation of my countenance. (Ps 42:6)

And you

If these feelings ever threaten your soul, take the Lord up on his invitation: "Come to me, all you grown weary and burdened, and I will refresh you. Take my yoke upon you and learn from me, for I am gentle and humble-hearted, and you will find rest for your souls. For my yoke is easy, and my burden light" (Mt 11:28–30). Who better than Jesus knows the value of human suffering? For our salvation he shouldered it all, even our sins.

21

Crank It Up!

Meek

Sometimes virtues are so subtle in themselves that we totally miss them. Meekness is one of these overlooked virtues. When we have it we think it's a defect to be corrected, and when we lack it we may entirely miss the point of this beatitude. The "meekless" might think this beatitude pertains only to big occasions, like being born in a stable or dying on a cross, not to common, everyday occurrences. For example, with me the problem is being ever so crabby. The family says that I always was a complainer; early on, neighbors would call about the baby's constant whining. It seems I was born to be irritated.

Perhaps we need Jesus to spell out the specifics. This happened one day when I was happily grousing about the situation of the bread table in the convent dining room. It's a large space with two big toasters, a substantial bread bin, a cutting board, a large bread knife, an assortment of jars containing peanut butter, jellies, butter, and the like. When I clean it off after meals, I find knives with jelly or butter lying all around the table. And so, I feel impelled to crab about it—aloud, of course, for what good is social commentary if no one hears it? This particular day as I waxed eloquently about the disorder, I heard the gentle Jesus begin his own commentary. "I notice you are concerned about the butter knives again," said Jesus. "Consider this: 1) You have butter *and* something to put it on; 2) You do not live alone; 3) People always leave a mess around my table of life; and 4) I've given you the power of observation and the ability to pray, so try to channel your frustration into prayer for the others." Well, count me blessed! Needless to say, whenever a crabby comment escapes my mouth now, I try to convert it to prayer.

We pray that you will be strengthened with all the power of his glorious might so that your steadfastness and patience will be perfected and you may joyfully give thanks to the Father who made you worthy to share in the portion of the saints in light. (Col 1:11–12)

And you

Whether your inclination is to *crank it up* or to indulge in some other non-virtuous behavior, are you praying to understand God's ways?

Thin Ice

Meek

As kids, when our actions were particularly annoying, my dad would say, "Okay, now you're skating on thin ice!" I don't think we knew the exact nature of the threat. All I knew of thin ice was the frozen slush in the neighborhood gutters. When you stepped off the sidewalk and the ice gave way, you might sink in icy water up to your ankles. Unless you had your boots on, you would get quite a chill and, more than likely, a bad cold would follow.

Now as an adult I understand the seriousness of actually skating on thin ice on a river or pond. Falling through would be perilous indeed. Anything from pneumonia to death could be your fate.

Today, with the constant barrage of electronic news reports, we are much more aware of the peril of our very existence, not only from accidents in the air, on land, or at sea; or from terrorists or unbalanced gun-toters; but also from our very Mother Earth herself. It seems that every week we hear a new report of another larger, more unpredictable volcano somewhere. In addition, earthquakes, fires, droughts, sinkholes, and pestilence abound. We are feeling ever so fragile. Then, of course, we face threats from both our stable and unstable celestial fellow citizens—the asteroids, solar flares, and so forth.

The beatitudes deal with an equally dangerous situation. Blessed are the meek for they shall inherit the earth. Meekness is necessary to preserve us from the natural disaster of our own anger. Our nature is so designed that we come with the necessary safety mechanism to prevent angry outbursts. It is true that some folks do have some equally natural impediments to the successful exercise of this virtue. Most of us, however, need only to understand the meaning and value of meekness.

> *"Blessed are the meek,*
>   *for they shall inherit the earth." (Mt 5:5)*

And you

In order to inherit, one needs to be willing to claim a certain ownership. An inheritance is wasted on one who is unwilling to exercise his or her newly acquired rights (and duties). If you have a hold on the gift of meekness, are you able to appreciate the mastery it allows you over your whole being?

23

Porpoise's Purpose

Meek

What's the purpose of a porpoise? Isn't that a great question? Do they really have to have a purpose? Porpoises are amazing swimmers and good communicators among themselves. Some have been known to protect humans disoriented at sea. But, as for a purpose—from our perspective—perhaps it's just to awe us and draw us to their Creator. It seems God may have made them simply for joy. They praise him and they also make us happy.

The same could be said of some virtues. On the surface they don't seem to have any positive purpose. For example, let's take the virtue of meekness. Acquiring meekness isn't on the bucket list of many folks. It isn't a desirable asset in the world as we know it. So, does meekness have a useful purpose? Well yes, it does, first of all because it's a virtue, that is, a characteristic of man, and in this case a particularly manly characteristic. We're not talking about weakness, but of meekness. Meekness requires strength and self-control. To practice it well a person needs self-mastery.

We admire proficiency in martial arts. Why? Because of the self-mastery required. Meekness is the same thing, and Jesus is the master's Master in this regard. He displayed this virtue of meekness many times, but never more evidently than during his Passion. Jesus was not just a man hauled unjustly to court. He was worthy of every sign of reverence and respect as the God-Man, the long-awaited Messiah, and our Redeemer. He was offering himself as expiation for the sins of all of us—something totally free and uncalled for, definitely something undeserved. Yet, he was passed around, mistreated, and insulted by crude and incompetent men. He, the Lord of all, was made sport of and publicly shamed. His purpose was all about us—out of love for us, and without regard for himself, he paid the price of our redemption.

> *He was led like a sheep to the slaughter,*
> *and as a lamb is silent before its shearers,*
> *he opened not his mouth. (Acts 8:32; see Is 53:7)*

And you

Who would have had more reason to defend himself than Jesus? He said he could have called on legions of angels to rescue him, but his purpose was our salvation. His strength was his meekness. Are you able to appreciate this degree of self-mastery? Think of occasions when meekness would strengthen you.

Meekest Man

Meek

Sacred Scripture tells us that Moses was the meekest man on the face of the earth (see Num 12:3). If that were so, why did God choose Moses to lead the people of Israel out of Egypt? The whole thing should have failed (and nearly did, humanly speaking). Years earlier Moses' courage was aroused and he attacked a man who was mistreating a Jew. Moses ended up killing the attacker. Moses' courage disappeared and so did he, into the desert. God, however, noted Moses' desire to protect the Chosen People, and during Moses' exile God purified his servant. Before the phenomenon of a bush afire but unconsumed, God laid out his plan. Not a hero by nature, Moses hesitated, not in accepting the charge but in envisioning how he would carry it out. So God assigned Moses' siblings, Aaron and Miriam, to accompany him as his spokespersons when he confronted Pharaoh. Despite his underwhelming natural presence, Moses was able to present the Lord's case to Egypt: "Let my people go!"

Moses was also able to perform dreadful signs and wonders before the eyes of the Pharaoh, which convinced the ruler to let the Jews go out to the desert on a pilgrimage. After their escape and the parting of the Red Sea at Moses' command, the people of Israel outran the Egyptian army just as the waters overwhelmed the enemy. Despite such a show of God-given power, the people nearly died in the desert basically from rebellious hearts. They wanted more from God and Moses than what was given.

When the people complained and demanded more water, God told Moses to hit a certain rock once and God would reveal a stream of drinkable water. But Moses added a stroke to God's directive, hitting the rock twice. Because he appeared to doubt God's word and did it publicly, God imposed a public punishment on his prophet: Moses would not lead the people into the land of promise. Moses recognized his failing and didn't argue his case or present reasons why he was only enhancing God's message. He meekly accepted his fault and its consequences.

Now the man Moses was very humble, more so than anyone else on the face of the earth. (Num 12:3)

And you

Moses brushed off personal praise, even saying that he wished all the people were prophets like himself. Are you able to accept both praise and reprimand with graceful equanimity?

Landowner

Meek

Occasionally I take a short detour into the online real estate section—not that I'm planning to purchase a home, but I love to see beautiful, well-appointed spaces, the pricier the better. I think every soul harbors a desire to own something unique and special. Some folks are wealthy enough to buy vast chunks of real estate, while average folks usually "own" mortgaged property through the good graces of their bank.

Jesus tells us, or rather promises us, that if we're meek we will inherit the earth. *Have to think about that one,* we say. *Perhaps there would be too much lawn to mow or too many snowy walkways to shovel.* What he's actually promising us is self-possession. Our bodies really are *earth*; in the Book of Genesis we see the first man being made from the earth, and at death our bodies return to the earth. This possession over our own *earth* isn't just mastery over our stronger inclinations, like anger and greed, but even over our weaker inclinations, like discontent and dissipation. In other words, by taking possession of who we are by birth—that is, our physical attributes, looks, disposition, intelligence, stamina, character, and so forth—we actually own what has been given us in this earthly existence. In this way we'll be grateful for everything we've received and be eager to accomplish whatever God wills in our lifetime.

When Jesus said, *Learn from me for I am meek and humble of heart*, he wasn't just stating some pious platitude. He meant it. Jesus knew who he was as Son of God; however, he put this aside in order to carry out our redemption. Jesus knew who he was as man: a poor laborer, the son of a carpenter, from a despised area, called to be our teacher, with a destiny of bitter suffering and death. He took possession of his identity in meekness, that is, in gentle humility of heart.

Rock-solid stronghold of my heart, my sole possession,
God of all eternity, in you my body and my mind are
both fulfilled. (Ps 73:26)

And you

Do you lose time and energy pining over what you don't possess? Set aside a few moments each day to be grateful for who you are by nature and nurture. Ask God to show you how to embrace his gifts and to always do his will.

Getting a Handle

Meek

Lots of useful items have handles: kettles, car doors, cabinets, purses, and bicycles, to name a few. Not long ago we had a car with handles for cranking the windows up or down. Yes, there are still cars with manually operated windows. But the handle for the driver's window was broken. Although it was great as an exercise routine, this inconvenience made everyday occurrences frustrating. The driver had to open her door to take a parking garage ticket, to ask directions, to adjust her side mirror (also manual), and to pay for and pick up drive-through meals. "Why didn't you just get it fixed?" you might ask. Well, only our bookkeeper knows for sure. But the point is that this problem caused frustration.

Something similar can occur in the personal realm as well. We all know people who lament because they can't seem to get a handle on their difficulties. One such difficulty might be fondly called "beaver speak." You know: "Damn this" and "Damn that." These folks generously bestow damnation as if it were a blessing. Soap in the mouth isn't the answer. Meekness is needed.

Often the practice of a virtue like meekness will become a real workout. We can hear God saying, "That was good, but let's do it again." It might help to open the Gospel and look for examples of Jesus' meekness. Pope John Paul I said that Jesus was the epitome of gentleness, kindness, and courtesy. In Luke 5:3, Jesus turns to Peter and says, "Would you please do me the favor of moving your boat out a-ways?" Jesus had stepped into the boat to put a bit of distance between himself and the crowd that was pushing against him while he spoke. He could have just rapped on the side of the boat and said, "Move it out!" However, he knew that meekness doesn't just exist on the inside but must also be evidenced in action.

> *But I said, "I have labored in vain,*
> *I have spent my strength for nothing and vanity;*
> *yet surely my cause is with the LORD,*
> *and my reward with my God." (Isa 49:4 NRSV)*

And you

Meekness offers a blessing when things go awry. Do we have any reason to expect a charmed life? Instead of getting all hot and bothered and sweating the small (or not so small) stuff, use the moment for praise and blessing.

In Flight

Justice (Hunger and Thirst)

Blessed are those who hunger and thirst. This beatitude seems an apt theme for modern air travel. You're running late for your flight. You dash in from the taxi to the terminal and run the gauntlet through security. Your first pause: realizing that had your primary care physician accompanied you for the full body scan, you could have saved time and money later on. You continue your marathon to the boarding gate, only to find that you forgot to pick up provisions for your trip. So, while you may land safely, you will be parched and famished.

If we could only feel that ravenous for holiness! *Blessed are those who hunger and thirst to do God's will, for they shall have their fill.* In other words, God will not be outdone in generosity. If we're literally consumed with the desire to please God, he will in turn fulfill our desires. This is the promise. The timing is iffy, however, because fulfillment comes in the future. This is probably for the best, because during our lifetime we're in search of God's will. We find it every now and then, yet it often manages to elude us. Scripture offers many examples of how God appears to change his mind about what he wants. Our Lady, for one, was secure in thinking God wanted her to remain a virgin, but then he sent a messenger. Gabriel, the Archangel, announced that God wanted her to be the mother of his own Son. God didn't exactly explain this new direction, but it was his will. Mary said her "yes."

Even Jesus, on the night before he died, begged his Father to change his mind about the approaching suffering. It had seemed he'd have more time to preach and cure and win hearts over to the loving plan of God, but the winds of change overcame him. The enemy was approaching. An agonizing death loomed. Jesus concluded his prayer in peace: "Not my will, Father, but yours be done." That God's will may prevail is the burning desire of God's holy ones.

> *I take delight, my God, in doing what pleases you,*
> *and your Law is at the very heart of my being.*
> *(Ps 40:9)*

And you

How hungry are you to know what God wants of you? Do you seek refreshment in prayer and in reading Scripture?

Mighty Waters

Justice

"Let justice roll down like mighty waters and righteousness like an ever-flowing stream" (Am 5:24).

One day in late November the waves at the lighthouse near our home were driven by two opposing storms. The waves smashed against each other in a seeming battle to reach the shore. The huge, broiling waves crashed into each other, and like downed fighters, got up, regrouped, and pounded in to shore. This is God's justice—relentless and powerful, constant and pure.

A fair-sized stream in town runs down to the waterfront and empties into the sea. It, too, is a constant but calmer power. Both the ocean and the stream are symbols of God's ultimate power, which is love. And love is also a driving force both within and outside of us. This power of love is found in the Gospel, in the words and example of Jesus.

"It can happen, however," notes Father S. Joseph Krempa, "that the plain words of Jesus in the Sermon on the Mount can be reduced to a heavenly ideal. The teachings of Jesus while he was in the flesh have a binding character on all Christians. When we overlook them, we are effectively denying that God came in the flesh. A Christian cannot have an a la carte spirituality. Jesus' teaching binds us in our politics, in our economics, and in our ambitions. Jesus did not give us a set of heavenly ideals but an earthly way of life."[1]

In addition to poverty, meekness, purity, and mercy, the disciple of Christ must practice justice, which is the righting of situations, and righteousness, which is the righting of our heart. Therefore, all areas of life will be driven by what is right and just in God's eyes.

> *Righteousness will precede him,*
> *and he will make his footprints into a way. (Ps 85:14)*

And you

Because Jesus was one of us in every way except our penchant for sin (see Heb 4:15), he can expect us to model all aspects of our lives on his. The Gospels show us many examples of Jesus dealing with very real human situations, including with the powerful and matters of economics. Take a few moments to let Jesus peek at your political leanings, your practical views on economics, and your personal ambitions. Can you imagine that Jesus will have any advice for you?

29

Without a Paddle

Justice

It doesn't take much rattling around in our own history to find instances when our folks had to at least attempt some significant punishment for childhood transgressions. For me it was the day my dear old Dad (who wasn't very old then) presented me with one-third of his belt. My sister and brother received matching gifts. Dad's greatest weakness was that he wasn't a disciplinarian. When it came to enforcing some law and order, he was literally down a creek without a paddle. So he came up with the idea to apportion out his belt to his oldest three darlings. We were to keep our piece in our dresser drawers for the moment of need. Did he ever resort to this dire punishment? I only remember being pointed to that drawer twice. "Okay, get ready. I'll be right there," Dad said. Then eventually and unconvincingly he would knock on the door and come in as the reluctant executioner of justice.

Parents are the greatest victims of these scenarios. "I'm doing this for your own good. It hurts me more than it hurts you." Under our breath we mumble, "Yeah, right!" We do get it eventually after reflection, especially after having to apply the justice/love argument to someone significant to us.

In meting out justice, I think Dad eventually took the same stance that God takes. God is perfectly just and unquestionably loving; he is willing to wait us out. Will we come to our senses and accept that he knows best and then throw ourselves on his love?

> *Children, obey your parents [in the Lord], because it is the right thing to do. Honor your father and mother! This is the first commandment that comes with a promise—that all may be well with you and you may have a long life on earth. And fathers, don't cause your children to resent you; instead, raise them by instructing and admonishing them as the Lord would. (Eph 6:1–4)*

And you

Now that you are an adult, do you maintain a sense of discipline? Certain rules and regulations in life are just there and they are inescapable. But in your own affairs, do you maintain a quiet vigilance?

Queen of Burgers

Justice

It was almost 8:30 PM and we hadn't stopped for supper.
So we picked a wide street that led into the center of town to
find some fast-food. Strangely, aside from the bars, everything seemed closed. Then we spied a magical neon sign
announcing fried chicken and burgers. We swung into the
nearest parking space and made a beeline for the door. Since
this place was obviously within our means, we checked the
menu. My three companions ordered chicken or salads while
I, the queen of hamburgers, ordered what I hoped was a classic. We retired to a booth and waited for what seemed to be a
good chunk of eternity. At last the man who had taken our
orders arrived with the food. The salads looked good, the
chicken appeared adequate, but the burger was nowhere to
be seen. Oddly, the bun was present, but it seemed empty. I
picked up the lid and, lo and behold, there was nothing to lo
and behold. Laying on the bottom half of the bun was a doily
of blackened grease. This one-dimensional beauty was my

burger. At that moment the owner arrived, delighted to find guests. He asked if everything was satisfactory, but when queried about the meatless hamburger he seemed surprised. "That's how we receive them from our supplier," he said. "I'll get you a second one if you'd like." To myself I was thinking, *I'd actually like to have the first one*, but I said, "No, no. This is fine. I'm satisfied." Really I was more stupefied, but there's no beatitude for that, so we finished eating and left.

When we are hungry or thirsty it is fairly easy to meet the need, but when we are speaking, as Jesus in the Gospel, of a consuming desire for justice, it is not such a simple matter. Our principal concern for justice is not self-centered, but that righteousness may prevail in our world. We want the lives of everyone to be protected and respected, God's world to be cared for and preserved, and God's laws to be appreciated and followed by all.

> *He loves righteousness and justice;*
> *the earth is full of the LORD's loving kindness. (Ps 33:5)*

And you

Is your righteousness generous and loving? If so, you will find you're satisfied even now by the grace of God poured into your heart.

Eau du Sheep

Justice

Have you ever tried to imagine the Christmas scene before Mary and Joseph arrived? I'm thinking of the back lot of the local Bethlehem inn—the field where the travelers parked their burros and where the innkeeper housed his own menagerie of sheep, cows, and chickens. That field was probably quite "icky." It would be full of. . . . Well, you know what it would have been full of. Into this field—in the dark— came Joseph leading Mary, who was hopefully still atop their donkey. The little shed couldn't have been any more decorous than the field, but it provided a degree of shelter for the babe about to be born. Something had to be spread out for Mary to lie on. So they sanitized the place and sprayed it with fresh linen air spray—NOT! The place definitely smelled of sheep, cows, birds, and mice, but how appropriate a birthplace for the Good Shepherd. Jesus came and remained ever in the midst of his people. As his assistant shepherds of today we, too, need to feel comfortable with the eau du sheep, as

Pope Francis noted; we should smell like the sheep. We need to learn the fine art of mingling with our contemporaries, starting with the near and dear. We know the smell of the culture they embody; we know the scent of their fears and preoccupations. It is imperative to feel real pangs of hunger and thirst to bring them to Jesus. This is the justice the Lord requires of us. We must labor to make things right, to bring the Kingdom with us wherever we go. But we can only accomplish this sacred trust by appreciating what it means to be truly companions to our contemporaries. It is not unrealistic to become good shepherds for those in need.

> *"And when he finds it he puts it on his shoulders, rejoicing, and when he comes home he calls his friends and neighbors together and says to them, 'Rejoice with me—I've found my lost sheep.'" (Lk 15:5–6)*

And you

You may find in your lifetime that you have had to hoist on your shoulders several lost or needy sheep. You're doing mercy, but it's a matter of justice as well. Things are made right when you act mercifully, when you do lovingly what calls out to be done.

All's Fair

Justice

The actual saying is "all's fair in love and war." Of course, as Christians, we don't buy into the fairness of war. And when we say all's fair in love, we don't buy into that idea either. However, we do believe all is fair in divine love. God has the Prophet Ezekiel lay it out for us: "If a wicked man converts, then nothing of his past is remembered. However, if a just man turns to evil, none of his good deeds will be remembered" (Ez 18:21–28). This doesn't sound right to us. We cry foul; God isn't playing fair!

Shall we ask then: What is fairness? In "weather-speak" a fair day is neither glorious nor miserable. It is right there in the good zone. What about the fair damsel of fairy tales? She possesses the attractive charm of youth, but is not a femme fatale. In this middle ground, then, all is fair.

According to Jesus, God doesn't operate out of fairness. He knows the right order of things and acts out of justice. But when it comes to us, his children, he acts out of mercy. Mercy is God's preferred brand of fairness. As a believer, Jesus states, we must be righteous beyond those who do everything rightly. In fact, if someone has something against you, you cannot continue even doing what you should do (like offering praise to God) without first going to seek reconciliation with that person. Why? Because Jesus, a man like us (in everything but sin), freely took upon himself all the sins of humankind and won forgiveness for us.

According to Caryll Houselander: "We must be just not because we are judges, for that we are not; but because we are trustees of God's love to the world, and justice is a supreme expression of his love. Justice belongs to God, it is a tender expression of his tenderness and pity."[1]

Let's make it our aim to be the Christ-like dispensers of mercy to all who cross our path each day. It is right; it is just; it is fair.

Is my way unfair? Is it not your ways that are unfair? (Ezek 18:25 NRSV)

And you

How do you deal with a God who is set in his ways? Fortunately for us his way is mercy, and the name of his way is Jesus. Do you always try to walk in God's ways?

33

Mercy Now Playing

Mercy

Last time I was at the dentist I thought the best use of my fearful anticipation would be to read a scholarly book on the Gospels. That was a bad idea. It was not calming at all, nor could I concentrate on it. A gaggle of cute little kids was noisily jumping and jostling one another, folks constantly went in and out, and all the time a large flat-screen TV was blaring the news: "Twenty-four were killed on pilgrimage; kidnapping victims are pleading for rescue; nations are threatening and counter-threatening nuclear destruction; death and desperation followed an early morning earthquake; pathetically narcissistic young men are accused of killing another fellow for disrespecting them." All this made the commercials sound like good news. Meanwhile, personal drama was playing out in the far corner of the waiting room, where a lovely young woman was trying to convince her significant other, via cell phone, that she was indeed at the dentist office.

How could I possibly concentrate on studying *about* the Gospel while it was being lived out, or not, before my eyes? How obvious it is that we all need Jesus and his Good News! It isn't just the big stories that underscore this need, but also the daily mini-dramas in which you and I play a starring role. How often have I been the lead story of the evening news at home? Whom did I hurt? What were those awful words I said? Am I ultimately the reason the two of us haven't made up yet? Mercy isn't a magical potion; it has to be a way of life.

"I am overcome with pity for the crowd. . . ." (Mt 15:32)

And you

Often the crowd calling for our pity and mercy are those we learn about in the news media. We don't watch the world's sorrows and struggles simply out of curiosity. If nothing else, we owe these real people our real prayers. More often than not, however, those with a claim on our mercy are the folks with whom we share life: family, friends, relatives, co-workers, store clerks, etc. Can you easily reach out in care and kindness? Notice in Matthew 16 that Jesus asked his disciples to help him show divine mercy to the hungry crowd. Every day he asks you and me to be the means by which he shows his loving mercy now.

Knock, Knock

Mercy

As adults we may lovingly listen to a favorite child's endless repertoire of "knock, knock" jokes. Less lovingly we endure the actual knocking on our door or the virtual knocking on our personal screens or phones. How often we call out: "Go away and leave me alone!" It seems we never have a moment of peace. Someone always wants something. It's like the man in the Gospel whose friend knocked on his door in the middle of the night. The friend needed bread for someone who dropped by unannounced. "I can't help you. We're all in bed. Go away," the man replied. But his friend persisted until the man got up and gave him what he requested. This happens to us as well. At any hour of the day or night our Friend, the Man of the Gospel, may be standing at our door knocking. He doesn't make it easy for us, however. We may not recognize him; his voice will be unfamiliar. He's easy to ignore. Well, why doesn't he say, "Hey, it's Jesus. Can you give me a hand?" At least we'd know it was the Lord, and of course we'd open immediately. Isn't it unfair of him to just knock and expect a proper reception? In fact, Jesus could simply open the door and come in whenever he wants. He's God! He'd always be welcome!

"Behold, I am standing at the door and knocking. If anyone hears my voice and opens the door I will come in to him and eat with him, and he with me." (Rev 3:20)

And you

During World War II a woman risked her own life to save strangers from certain death. When her neighbors asked whatever possessed her to take such a chance, she replied, "They needed help and I was there." We may not feel that brave, but we must ask ourselves about the needy of our day. Their need may not be as dire, but they do need help and we are here. Can our excuse for not helping be that good?

We have endless opportunities to be merciful or to do a favor. You might want to look up the famous paintings by William Holman Hunt or Warner Sallman of Christ rapping on a door that has no outside handle. He can only be admitted from within. Reflect on the times Christ may stand at your door and knock.

The Gift of Mercy

Mercy

Most of the world admires Mother Teresa of Calcutta for the way she gifted herself to the poor. She offered her whole life as a way of showing God's love to those who had every human reason to doubt that God exists. She acted out the parable of the Good Samaritan, not only by taking in those who were left for dead, but also by searching for them. She was the Good Shepherd: seeking the lost and bringing them home. She brought them to realize that love does exist and that *they* are lovable, that each person is someone sought out by God.

This beatitude of mercy could also be called the blessing of social concern. The beatitude is about going out of my life and into the life of another. We know the nursery rhyme about Bo Peep, the little girl who had a few sheep but somehow lost track of them. She didn't seem overly concerned about them, however, and concluded that they would eventually come home wagging their tails behind them. That's all well and good in a rhyme, but in real life sheep don't automatically make it back to the fold. The beatitude of mercy offers us the incentive to express goodness toward others in imitation of Jesus, who came to seek and save what was lost. Those who belong to his fold (and that would be everyone) need to be on the lookout for one another, to be concerned for the safety and salvation of all the flock—especially those who have wandered off—but also to bring the love of God to those who have strayed far and fallen in with robbers who would steal from them any hope of returning.

> *"Amen, I say to you,*
> *insofar as you did it for one of these least of my brothers,*
> *you did it for me." (Mt 25:40)*

And you

Can you lobby for a cause—for example, better schools in poor areas, social services for the homeless, or jobs for young people; offer help with learning to read or studying for exams; assist the elderly with such things as mowing the lawn, making a trip to the store or an appointment, caring for the graves of their loved ones, or walking their dog? Acts such as these move mercy from the page into real life.

Mercy Mindset

Mercy

No one likes to be pitied, but we all love mercy. Pity makes us feel somehow weak, whereas mercy assures us that we are loved. We count on God's mercy. We hope the good Lord will overlook our sins and faults—all of them, especially, as we say in the *Confiteor*, "what I have failed to do": all those things we should have done, could have done, but didn't. These are the most unrelenting regrets.

Although mercy is natural to God, it isn't really something we so naturally offer. Mercy is what makes God *God*. It is who he is—"the Father of all mercy." We willingly accept God's pity because we recognize our misery before him. He is perfection and we, simply put, are not. In fact, we are naught—nothing, except by his giving. When we recognize this difference between God and ourselves, we also begin to see the likeness that exists. We are buoyed up, lightened, and lifted by the realization that God has made us—raised us from nothingness—in his image and likeness. He is also always ready to pump us up with more of this divine life—something we know as grace.

God sent his mercy in the Person of the Son. So in seeking to be more godlike, we begin by sharing the mercy given us—we send it out to others; bestow it freely, unreasonably, unreservedly, without measure or end. By praying the Chaplet of Divine Mercy we more easily assume the mindset of mercy.

Jesus didn't stay in Nazareth waiting for disciples to arrive. Rather, he left the comfort of home and sought them out. He became itinerant mercy, taking the Father's mercy on the road.

We must take his mercy with us on the road as well. Not that we need to canvas the face of the earth, but we are called to travel our own roads, bestowing mercy.

> *He traveled throughout all Galilee, teaching in their synagogues, proclaiming the good news of the Kingdom, and healing every disease and illness among the people. (Mt 4:23)*

And you

Why does the priest send us from Mass with this admonition: "Go in peace, glorifying the Lord by your life"? Not just to give us a personal sense of peace, but the peace born of mercy that now must be shared.

I Owe You

Mercy

One of the most compelling stories Jesus told is about the unforgiving servant. For some reason not revealed in the Gospel, this fellow had fallen on hard times. He owed an impossible amount to his creditor, who ordered him to be sold together with his whole family. The servant appears sincere when he begs for time. "I *will* pay back what I owe," he promises. The creditor, a reasonable, kindhearted man, realizes the bind the man is in and doesn't just grant more time, but entirely erases the debt. Imagine the relief! The man's whole world had almost caved in, but now all was light and free. We would expect him to run down the street hugging total strangers with his new lease on life, but not so. Jesus tells us that this newly forgiven man runs into an acquaintance who owes him a fraction of the debt that was just written off. He grabs this man, demanding payment. We are aghast at this turn of events, but it worsens. This minor debtor falls on his knees and pleads for patience. He is trying his best; he will fulfill his promise and pay back his debt. But no, the servant orders him to be arrested and thrown into prison, along with his wife and children, until he can pay back what he owes. That's crazy, we say, how can anyone repay a debt from behind bars? All of this is soon reported back to the generous creditor, who immediately reinstates the claim he erased. The unforgiving servant is then thrown into prison, and a collective hooray goes up from all who've ever read the story. What a foolish, insensitive, insincere reaction he had to another who shared his misfortune. How could he not forgive in turn?

How often are we that man? We do wrong, we offend, and we beg forgiveness. People are good, and, more often than not, they willingly forgive in response to a sincere request. God, for his part, always and unconditionally forgives us when we ask to be forgiven. The question remains: How forgiving are we of others?

> *"Shouldn't you have had mercy on your fellow servant, too, as I had mercy on you?" (Mt 18:33)*

And you

Develop a merciful heart, empathy for others. Put yourself in another's place and exercise the divine prerogative of mercy in all situations of life, whether important or insignificant.

Merci Me

Mercy

If I know how to ask for mercy, I'm more capable of bestowing mercy. But mercy isn't just pardon of offenses and commuting of punishment. Mercy is the tone of our existence. The mercy of God shown through Jesus Christ, who is himself Divine Mercy, makes us Christian.

Each day brings many mercies to bestow. *Treat others as you would be treated*, Jesus said. How is this translated into daily life except through the unexceptional? Do I show my thanks for a kindness, no matter how slight—even to a total stranger? Someone pushes into a very long line, mumbling, "I'm late. I beg your pardon. Hate to cut in, but I'm in a hurry." If you're like me, it's so tempting to reply, "Well, so am I. Get back in line!" Thank God for good old human respect, which so often masks our threadbare virtue.

When it's our turn and we need to get somewhere quickly, do we try to inconspicuously insert ourselves, thinking the "rule" is never to make eye contact? How much more pleasant life would be if we could rely on common courtesy. We have a whole vocabulary to support everyday mercy: *may I, thank you, excuse me, forgive me, pardon me, allow me, certainly, and, of course, bless you*—to list a few.

These simple expressions of mercy prepare us to cope with the bigger, more burdensome calls for mercy-giving. If we open our hearts and use our tongue to convey kindness, we won't be caught unaware by sudden calls for mercy.

"Mercy," says Simon Tugwell, "is no soft option. It is not a matter of conniving or finding excuses. It is the only really hard-headed response to evil, faced frankly and judged accurately for what it is. It is the only power that can face evil and not flinch, because it knows a power stronger than evil, the power of God's Word, in which the promise of creation still stands, and in which, therefore, the seed of new creation waits to germinate."[1]

"Be merciful, as your Father is merciful." (Lk 6:36)

And you

Jesus promised that whatever we do for the least of his brothers and sisters, we do to him. All God's children are Jesus' brothers and sisters, although at times we are tempted to number as "least" those who offend us. Therefore, freely show and bestow mercy.

Driven Snow

Pure of heart

"Pure as the driven snow" is a quaint saying, written prior to the grimy slush of the automotive era. But it's still a beautiful metaphor for virtue and the state of purity. Many today appear to value purity only as a "give-away": early and often. "Well," one might huff, "it is *my* body, after all!" Yes, it is your body, which is all the more reason to jealously protect it. People use their bodies as if they were replaceable commodities. Actually more than just your body is at stake; it's also your personal integrity, your very "self"—body and soul—or if your prefer not to have a soul, your body and *spirit*.

Possess your YOU, body and spirit, fiercely, tenaciously, and tenderly until you are ready to surrender it freely and forever in marriage to that one person you cannot live without. And here is another precise word: when we give our *self* so completely to another, it is not just our *without* but also our *within* that we are sharing. A proof of this comes to light when a child is born: he or she possesses not just the physical traits but the spiritual traits of both parents.

Don't buy into a marketplace morality with its buying and selling, constant comparisons, and trial runs with numerous "lovers." Somehow these lovers come without any warranty but with a return policy. "If you aren't completely satisfied, we'll return your money in full." Remember, however: a service charge is always levied.

Blessed be purity! No one likes to do "snow angels" in roadside slush; we prefer pure driven snow—newly fallen, undisturbed, awaiting our embrace.

I give you thanks for the terrific wonder that I am!
        Your works are wonderful
        and my spirit knows it too well.
My bodily frame was not hidden from you
        when I was being made in the secret recess,
        when I was being interwoven in the depths of the
            earth. (Ps 139:14–15)

And you

One way to look at the blessing that comes from the sixth beatitude is this: a pure heart allows you to see God within your own self, body and soul, the whole you. Baptism tells us that God lives within us, but to realize that you yourself, as you are, are an image of God is truly amazing. Take time to reflect on the wonder that you are, and bless your Creator.

40

Face to Face

Pure of heart

We have all heard of dancing cheek-to-cheek, but the sixth beatitude promises more: that we will find ourselves *face to face* with God. We shall see God. What do we hope that will mean? Perhaps our obsession with our own appearance is a nod to a belief that we are the image of God. We do not see our God in this life, but we see our own image and it fascinates us. Beauty, of course, is another matter and is pretty much dictated by whatever is in vogue. For example, in bygone centuries a woman with more substance, shall we say, was considered beautiful. This standard of beauty was immortalized by painters such as Rubens. In certain cultures, moles are seen as distinguishing marks of beauty, whereas we try to eliminate even the slightest imperfection. Some people prefer a very pale complexion, while others spend hours in tanning salons seeking a richer tone. Not many of us are really oblivious to our own looks. We may be only tolerant of what we received from the gene bank and have tried to enhance it over the years.

Our true image, however, is not just outer beauty, but our inner truth and goodness as well. The heart is a treasure house. We model our human love life on this divine program: blessed are the single-hearted. Beauty is truly in the eye of the beholder. When it comes to the beatitude, however, beauty is also in the one beheld. We will see him face to face. He will be gazing at us as we behold his eternal beauty.

> *"Do not look on his appearance or on the height of his stature, because I have rejected him; for the LORD does not see as mortals see; they look on the outward appearance, but the LORD looks on the heart. (1 Sam 16:7)*

And you

How do you imagine you will come to see God's face? The beatitude promises this reward to the pure of heart. Is your understanding of this statement limited to matters of sexual integrity?

Unsightly

Pure of heart

"Can you see that? What does it say?" This used to be me. Every few minutes I'd be straining to read something that seemed clear to everyone else. First thing I'd do was check my glasses. All smudgy, right? So off they'd go through the mini hand-version of a car wash: squirt, squeegee, polish. I'd put them back on all sparkly and clean, but . . . oh, my, I still couldn't see clearly.

At last I made an appointment and hauled myself off to the eye doctor, who, after careful and extensive examination, declared that I had cataracts. After further appointments and a surgery, I could once again see everything clearly. No more yellowish cast marred my sight. In fact, colors were a riot of hues and tones with a clarity I don't ever remember being aware of before.

Clear-sightedness is the blessing of the sixth beatitude as well. It says that the pure of heart will see so well that they will be able to see God. Do we object: "How can that be, since

God is a spirit and spirits aren't visible?" That's true about God; he is an invisible spirit, but we share in this spiritual world as beings composed of body and soul. God is everywhere; he is all around us and even within us. Our spirit can "see" God, but we have to keep our spirit clean of smudges and not allow a smog of inattentiveness to settle in. Distractions create the smudges and stains, and sins, large and small, form a discoloring film over the spirit. We can become so used to this condition—just as with a cataract that clouds the vision of our eyes—that we don't even notice the problem.

"What do you want me to do for you?" "Lord," he said, "please let me see again!" (Lk 18:41)

And you

The corrective treatment for spiritual cataracts is similar to the care we give our eyes. If God is an obscure concept, perhaps you should check up on your idea of God, first of all. However, if many other things stand in the way of your clear view of God, you need to take serious stock of your priorities and interests. The impediment can be sin, and then a little soul surgery known as the Sacrament of Reconciliation will do the trick. Take a serious peek at your priorities today.

Hippopotamouse

Pure of heart

It lurked in the dark recesses above my drop ceiling. Every night I heard it pacing and pouncing. Could it be that my worst fear was true? What if it came into my room? My companions shared knowing looks when I described what I heard. "But I know something is up there!" I cried. Finally, after enduring my interminable whining, one brave soul climbed up and gingerly laid a couple of traps. The scampering became more desperate that night, then silence. Next morning, as the body was removed, I nervously stood by, eyes tightly shut. Even though I didn't peek, I'm positive my nightly tormentor was the horrid hippopota*mouse*—the biggest, baddest bedroom beast ever. Now, I must admit the size and ferocity of my ceiling visitor was somewhat exaggerated, but at least it was gone.

Sometimes we don't seek a savior from our inner tormentors. For example, an imaginary figure may stalk our sleeping hours and, while we don't want to entertain the thought, we can't get rid of the phantom. What makes us so reticent about such torments? "It's a temptation, that's why! What would others think if they knew I had *temptations*?" Well, they'd list you under "perfectly normal," and although there's no need to share, a good rule of normalcy is to confide in someone, for example, one's confessor or spiritual director.

Purity of heart assumes that what troubles us is residing in our innermost recesses and isn't being acted out. While purity of heart covers far more territory than our inner struggles with temptations, this is a basic starting point. Innocent dreams of a romantic future are just that, and they are necessary preparations for sharing our hearts with that special one-and-only. However, our heart and imagination must be preserved from becoming a private porn shop. Remember that Jesus identified this invisible activity as sin: Whoever looks lustfully at a woman (or a man), commits adultery with her (or him) in their heart.

> *The person of stainless hands and upright heart,*
> > *whose soul does not yearn for emptiness*
> > *and who has not sworn deceivingly,*
> > *will draw blessings from the LORD*
> > *and approval from his saving God. (Ps 24:4–5)*

And you

This is a good place to ask yourself about your reading and viewing habits. Are you clear with yourself about what is helping you direct your heart toward holiness?

Chocolate Wars

Pure of heart

Could you survive a chocolate war? Some of you are hyperventilating and offering to give it a generous try. However, the real Chocolate War of 1973 did not involve hurling large semi-sweet cannon balls or jumping in trenches of this liquid gold. No, this war of the European chocolatiers involved most of the great names in the world of chocolate confection. The point of contention was this: Should lesser quality candy be allowed on shelves next to the traditional? Could vegetable oil replace cocoa butter? Would it then even merit to be called chocolate? Now the Europeans were pitted against one another: the purists and the potential folders. The fondues and the fondon'ts, you could say. The great chocolate makers wanted to offer the quality confections they were known for—not cheaper versions, no matter how profitable. The integrity of the chocolate bar was at stake. A truce was drawn up in 2003, allowing Europeans to choose their chocolates from less to best.

In the end the proof is in the pudding, as they say. Folks end up choosing by taste preference. If the bar satisfies our taste buds, the war has been won.

A similar good fight goes on all the time for the purity of our hearts. Jesus once said very clearly that we aren't defiled by what we take in, but by what comes out of our mouths (Mt 15:11). In other words, we should avoid all duplicity; we are to be sincere and upright, not self-absorbed or hypocritical but open-hearted with a clear conscience. We strive to be authentically Christian, undiluted and full-flavored.

Living in this authenticity makes it possible to see God not just in eternity, but also in all of his creation. We'll see God's pure being in the great and glorious—like majestic mountains—to tiny pleasures, like the cocoa bean.

Who is qualified, LORD,
> *to take up his abode in your tent,*
> *to dwell on your holy mountain?*
The one who lives uprightly,
> *who practices virtue,*
> *and is truthful to himself. (Ps 15:1–2)*

And you

It's hard to imagine eating baker's chocolate. Most of us really prefer something flavorful, such as bittersweet. We like our candy to be defined. Another rendering of the word *purity* calls it "single-heartedness." Is your heart set on being a purely unalloyed Christian?

Stringed Instrument

Pure of heart

As a teenager the voice of Joan Baez infatuated me. Her vocal range was mesmerizing, and her calls to social action touched my soul. Fortunately for me, God already had first dibs on me: I wanted to be a nun at all costs. Meanwhile, back in my adolescent life, I had decided to learn the guitar. I could carry a tune pretty well, but what good was that without the iconic guitar?

One morning my good friend Marcie, who lived on the first floor of our three-decker, mentioned how disillusioned she was with her guitar (who knew she even had one?). "I'm thinking of selling it," she mused.

"What a coincidence," said I. "You'll never guess what I'm hoping for."

"A guitar!" we said together.

We struck a deal, and I possessed a guitar. Then everything came up short: 1) I was short-sighted about my new "career"; 2) my enthusiasm for learning what turned out to be an eight-steel-stringed instrument was very short; and 3) my fingers were way too short to cross the span of strings. The finishing touch came when I realized my treasured guitar was out of tune. Well, that's what the little knobs on the top were for, right? The tighter the better, correct? Yes, I snapped a string, fortunately without killing myself. Such was my early career in music!

Sometimes our heart can come up short. It, too, is a stringed instrument that can get out of tune. Perhaps we have grand plans for our future, but the present gets in the way. In tuning up our heart, a string or two can be broken by a heartache, a disappointment in a relationship, or just a foolish mistake. What will restore that harmony of heart again?

Vigilance is needed. If your heart is a little bit here and a little bit there, it is more difficult to see God and follow his lead. Let God always be front and center. The single-hearted are always attuned to God.

> *Create a clean heart for me, O God,*
> *and renew within me an upright spirit. (Ps 51:12)*

And you

Have you ever mistreated your heart by carelessly stretching its chords, perhaps even breaking them? The music of life must go on. Where have you gone to restore your inner harmony?

XXXXXXX *45* XXXXXXXXXXXXXXXXXXXXXXXXXXXXXXXXXX

Imperfect Perfection

Peace

Many of us have settled, not unlike our pioneering fore-bears. Those hardy folks packed themselves into covered wagons and ventured into the wilderness where they set up homesteads. While surrounded by uncertainty, danger, and inconvenience, merely putting down roots constituted happiness for them. In our lives we often "settle" in the good sense. We dream of the perfect life, but as the years pass, we realize our definition of "perfection" is faulty.

During my childhood our family moved a number of times. Looking back, I realize that financial constraints caused most of those moves. My mother sometimes mentioned houses she had really loved—the spacious kitchen in one, the closet space in another, a porch here, a yard there—but the main concern of my parents was that the family could settle. With every move they had to slim down their original dream. The reality of life was never perfect, but what mattered was that we settled into life as a family.

Perfection doesn't need to be as perfect as planned.

I recently reconnected with a young man preparing to enter the Benedictines. Because candidates generally spend some time trying out the monastic life before being admitted, he prepared by working with the monastery's woodsman. Together they trimmed trees, dragged branches, and chopped logs. One day Brother Woodsman set up a conveyor belt to help pile the wood on their truck. He loaded the logs on one end and my friend was to catch and pile them. All went well until the brother increased the speed of the conveyor. My friend was scrambling and fumbling as he tried to collect the pieces coming at him. But then he said to himself: *I'm only going to do what I can*. In a few moments the woodsman shut the belt off and said to my friend, "Congratulations! You've passed the test. In our life we do not try to do everything to perfection, but to do it as well as we can in peace."

> *"Peace I leave with you,*
> *my peace I give to you;*
> *Not as the world gives*
> *do I give to you." (Jn 14:27)*

And you

What is your current definition of success? Are you driven by a false sense of perfection, or are you content to do well what is expected in a spirit of peace?

Amateur Thief

Peace

One afternoon in our Pauline Book Center I unlocked the display case and showed a couple of pieces to a customer who wanted a rosary bracelet for his daughter's graduation. I turned away a moment to help another person and looked back in time to see a bit of shine peek out of the man's sleeve. All kinds of virtual lights went off announcing: *Very amateur thief!* So when the man said that he would have to ask his wife about what to buy their daughter, I quietly mentioned that something might have accidentally slipped into his sleeve. He made a little show of checking and, sure enough, a gleaming bracelet slipped out. "Thank goodness you noticed that, Sister," he mumbled.

I was glad I could let my "thief" off the hook, but I imagine Jesus was so much happier to pardon the Good Thief on Calvary. Known to tradition as Dismas, he deserved the death sentence by his own admission. I like to think of Dismas as someone not unlike my thief; someone who got uncomfortably involved in crime because of some pressing necessity. Dismas seems to be a reflective, good-hearted man. The scene on Calvary confirms this. Jesus maintains an amazing peace despite his mortal agony. Dismas wants a share in that peace. Perhaps he had heard Jesus preach about the Kingdom, but certainly he had heard the stories of this preacher and his claims of connection with God and his reign. "Remember me when you come into your Kingdom," he calls over to Jesus. This is what Jesus was all about. He rises above his suffering to promise, "This day you will be with me in Paradise" (Lk 23:43).

What you have received from me, what you have learned, what you have heard, what you have seen in me, do these things, and the God of peace will be with you. (Phil 4:9)

And you

Dietrich Bonhoeffer warns that "there is no way to peace along the way of safety. For peace must be dared. It is the great venture. It can never be safe."[1] Dismas gained this insight as he observed the Prince of Peace face his death. Are you able to dare peace? Are you a spontaneous peacemaker?

The Power of One

Peace

As a kid I had a superpower complex. I guess I wasn't the typical frilly girly-girl. One of my favorite pastimes was "saving the day." Whenever a problem arose, I imagined myself solving it. I was kinder, smarter, and faster than anyone else, and I could even fly. I suspect this is a fairly common childhood fantasy. Interestingly, in my daydreams I never had a sidekick or associate; I operated solo.

Even as adults we often find ourselves dreaming of "saving the day," be it at home, at work, or in a crisis of global proportions. Some folks, such as the president, really do have responsibility to shepherd us through very serious international situations, and we often place unrealistic expectations on these elected officials.

Yet, despite heroic fantasy, how do we deal with our own inner turmoil? Do we cultivate inner peace? Do we allow civil war among our members? Do we aid and abet the enemy within? Think of what causes you to come undone. Do you fly off the handle, cower in tension, follow every whim, wallow in self-pity, envy the successful, distrust the generous, bully any sign of weakness, imagine offenses all around, strike out without provocation? The impulses of our spirit may not be at peace. We may act only on instinct and not on what are truly our superpowers when enhanced by grace, that is, our ability to reason and choose.

> *Don't have an exaggerated opinion of your own wisdom. Don't pay back evil with evil, set your sights on what all consider to be honorable. If possible live in peace with everyone to the extent that you're able to. (Rom 12:16–18)*

And you

Augustine says we cannot rule what is inferior to us unless we in turn are subject to the higher power, that is, to Truth itself, the Son of God. Latch on to the superpower of grace, which is yours for the asking. Jesus offers you himself as Way, Truth, and Life. He wants to reign in your mind as divine truth, in your will as divine strength, and in your heart as divine love. The truth of who you are to be is found in the perfect man, Jesus Christ, and shared in the gift of grace.

Nuttier Than

Peace

You guessed it! "Nuttier than a fruit cake"—an expression used in reference to less than stellar behavior. It describes crazy ideas and impossible scenarios. "Just the thought of someone single-handedly bringing about world peace is nuttier than a fruit cake."

I happen to love fruit cakes—real fruit cakes, not the pound cake stuffed with plastic fruit. Genuine fruit cakes require patience and attention to timing and detail. For example, it makes a difference when and if liquor is added. The kind and quality of fruit and nuts also matter, as does the baking and storage process. And the nuttier, the better.

When we look at the state of our world, at how many nations are at war, at the number of young children growing up in the midst of violence and hatred, the idea of a sudden peaceful solution seems absolutely nutty. We do not seriously imagine ourselves, or anyone else for that matter, brokering a mantle of peace that would cover the world. Some persons, however, have this mission: to help work out terms of peace amenable to all parties involved.

Most of us are called to be purveyors of peace on a more intimate scale. We realize that although peacemaking is not as cut and dry as a construction project, it is indeed like making a fruit cake: a long, involved process that requires attention, precision, patience, and a large dollop of love. Peacemaking is a living, breathing endeavor. Peace cannot be imposed or it will lack that genuineness that gives life. The sweet liquor of peace has to be love, or that peace will be a cheap, tasteless imitation doomed to fail. Pretending the pound cake with plastic fruit is a true fruit cake is as frivolous as identifying liking with loving. True peace does not require the attraction of friendship, the feeling we get when we like someone. True peace requires love, which is respectful, attentive, patient, forgiving, and kind.

Depart from evil and do good;
seek peace and follow after it. (Ps 34:15)

And you

Do you see yourself as a genuine peacemaker? Are you aware of the virtuous ingredients at your disposal for creating a peaceful atmosphere within your family or at your place of work? Are you ready for the time, attention, and patience required for true peace?

49

The Good Will Peace

Peace

Everyone on earth wants peace, although maybe not right away. The problem is we want it on our own terms. At Jesus' nativity, angels appear singing, "Glory to God in high heaven and on earth peace to men (and of course women) of good will." Here lies the catch: true peace must be sought for God's ultimate glory, and it's only achieved by those who are good. The good actually *will* peace; in other words, they put in a wholehearted effort to bring about peace. According to Thomas Merton, himself a lifelong seeker of peace, we're often mistaken in our pursuit of peace. We love the ideal of peace, but we overlook the opportunities to demonstrate peace by actual love of others. Instead of getting bent out of shape at the hatred we observe in someone else, we should identify those feelings and intentions deep within our own self that lead to injustice, greed, intolerance, or vengeance. Seek the causes of war first of all, Merton says, in our own soul.

This sentiment is found in the life of Saint Rita of Cascia, who would have been expected to demand some kind of revenge after a hit was put on her husband that also resulted in the death of her sons. Instead, Rita went to the rival family to offer forgiveness and peace. It was as if she knew these words of Henry Wadsworth Longfellow: "If we could read the secret history of our enemies, we should find in each man's life sorrow and suffering enough to disarm all hostility."[1]

Another surprising exemplar of this peacemaking spirit is Eustace Ahatsistari, a Huron chief and an early convert of the Jesuits known as the North American martyrs. In fact, Eustace was leading Isaac Jogues and others on the fateful day of their capture. Although Eustace suffered terrible torture at the hands of his enemies, he insisted that he wanted no vengeance. "I don't want my sufferings in any way to endanger the possibility of peace with the Iroquois."

Both Eustace and Rita were persons of good will or, better put, of godly will. They wanted only what God originally desired, that we all come into his peace.

Mark the honest man and watch the upright individual,
for there is a future for a man of peace. (Ps 37:37)

And you

Prayerfully reflect on the best peace this world offers as compared with eternal peace. Are you able to will good amid evil?

Harmony

Peace

Years ago we developed a slide program based on the writings of Blessed Pope Paul VI called *Peace: Where Is It?* The first thing on the menu of life, however, should be to know *what* peace is. According to Saint Gregory of Nyssa, "the definition of peace is harmony between two opposing factions."

"I would like some peace and quiet." We often hear these words at home, in the classroom, or at work, as if peace and quiet were synonyms. We seek peace of soul, the removal of guilt and anguish; peace in the midst of physical conflict and the senseless violence of our city streets; and peace to replace the constant destructive violence of international wars. The fortunate can snatch peaceful moments—sitting quietly with a cup of tea, rocking a beautiful sleeping baby, kneeling in adoration before the Blessed Sacrament. But snatching is only momentary; it's an interlude.

Why do we call the peace that reigns in a musical score *harmony*? It's the close collaboration among tones, which even cross and counter-point one another, that creates the *harmony*, the beautiful blending of sounds. But everyone must know their part well, have a feeling for the whole piece, sense the timing, and follow the director's lead.

In fact, with music we start the process of making peace each time a new score is learned.

So it is with the peacemaking that Jesus desires of us. Each of us must buy into the process of peacemaking; it always starts within the individual. In *A Treatise on Christian Perfection*, Gregory of Nyssa continues by saying: "It is when the civil war in our nature has been brought to an end and we are at peace within ourselves that we become peace. Then we shall really be true to the name of Christ that we bear."

> *May God, the source of hope, fill you with all joy and peace through your belief in him, so that you will overflow with hope by the power of the Holy Spirit. (Rom 15:13)*

And you

Peace doesn't just happen. It requires concentration, effort, and perseverance. Sometimes we have to keep restarting, but a peaceful spirit will win out. Do you trust the Holy Spirit to favor you with his gift of peace?

Worms

Persecuted

Nobody loves me; everybody hates me: I'm gonna eat some worms. As children we girls would jump rope to this little rhyme, while the boys latched onto the word "worms" and promptly chased us with the squirmy creatures dangling from a stick. As adults we sometimes believe the rhyme is true: "They're out to get me!" However, upon reflection we usually find this isn't exactly the case. We realize that the "they" we fear might just be the quirks in our social system. Sometimes, however, the unscrupulous are out to get the anonymous lot of humanity. We can "be had," as they say, in so many ways.

So it is perfectly normal and pretty common to feel a little persecuted. And in these cases we do well to advocate for our rights (and those of others, too).

Does persecution exist in our society? Yes, it does. At times people are profiled, bullied, picked on, harassed, and harangued. Sometimes the "persecutor" is a neighbor or a relative; other times it is law enforcement or a government agency, a passer-by or a total stranger. Harm could be perpetrated by the good, the bad, the malicious, or the indifferent. Jesus says: "Blessed are you when you are persecuted for doing good, for the Kingdom of heaven is yours." Nowhere does he stipulate that normal feelings can't precede or follow this blessedness. Jesus doesn't say that we can't be upset by the injustice of it all. We can and most likely will feel anger, dismay, fear, even vengefulness in some cases. But feeling is normal, forgiving is divine. When we take on the beatitudes, we are taking on Jesus. Better said, we are putting on Jesus like a garment of goodness.

> *Grace and peace be with you from God our Father and the Lord Jesus Christ, who gave himself for our sins to deliver us from the present evil age in accordance with the will of our God and Father, to whom be glory forever and ever. Amen! (Gal 1:3–5)*

And you

Try to think of this beatitude in positive terms. "Is that really possible?" you ask. "After all, it's speaking of persecution. How could any 'blessing' come out of that?" Try to envision your life from the perspective of the Kingdom. What possible injustice could happen in your lifetime that could outweigh eternal happiness?

52

Singing in the Reign

Persecuted

Music is used to ramp up scenes in films or TV programs. Like me, you may have toyed with possible music to accompany the scenes of your daily dramas; after all, we need to prepare for the filming of our bios!

Could your life actually become a full song-and-dance routine? Perhaps not, but it's nice to imagine life as a bit epic.

Some of us do provide occasional background music as we sing or hum a favorite tune to the rhythm of our daily life. We have walking music, working music; music for waking up and breaking up; for commuting, communing, consuming, and, of course, for singing in the shower. On solemn occasions or feast days we might even find ourselves singing something holy.

This was the case for Paul and Silas, two of the great New Testament missionaries. Their message of Good News didn't go over well with everyone in Antioch. They were arrested, publicly beaten, and unceremoniously chained in the prison's lowest dregs. Not the best of days! Yet, to the amazement of the other prisoners, it occasioned a praise and worship session for the two apostles. A strong earthquake suddenly interrupted all this, causing the cell doors to break open. All the prisoners should have skedaddled into the night, but they stayed, touched by the apostles' sincere melodies of praise.

We may be more than willing to sing through the good, better, and best moments of our lives and at least hum our way through the dimly lit moments, but are we able to sing out full-throated in times of trial and turbulence? What about when life itself seems like a persecution? As brothers and sisters of Jesus Christ, whose life and death resounded to the glory of God his Father, we learn to make our own lives a living hymn of praise. We are consciously bringing in the Kingdom. We could say that we are singing in the reign.

When he goes forth, the bearer of the seed to be scattered
    weeps as he goes;
    when he comes home, the bearer of his own
    sheaves comes shouting with joy. (Ps 126:6)

And you

For now songs are sung in the silence of your heart. Choose one that lifts your spirit—a song that stirs your very soul—and let it summon God's Kingdom within you.

53

Wrestling

Persecuted

My dad rarely watched television, except for Saturday night wrestling. Dad loved the collection of muscle-bound contestants with flamboyant names who threw each other around like rag dolls. "You know this is all show," he'd say. "There's no way they could keep it up without getting hurt."

In the Bible a real wrestling match takes place between Jacob and a mystery man (see Gen 32). Under cover of darkness Jacob was trying to ferry his family and their possessions away from the reach of his brother Esau. Years earlier, Jacob had deviously cheated his brother out of the paternal blessing due to the eldest son. Now Jacob was returning home, unsure of the welcome Esau would give him. Once everyone had safely crossed the river and Jacob stopped to catch his breath, a man appeared and challenged him to a fight. They struggled until dawn, when Jacob's hip was injured. The mystery man called a truce, but Jacob wouldn't give in until the man revealed his identity. The place where this happened is called Peniel, because there Jacob prevailed over, as it turned out, *God himself.* He wrestled a blessing from God by his perseverance.

Sometimes we find that we must wrestle with some inclination or fault that keeps us from the perfection we seek. The secret is perseverance. We may have to limp into paradise like Jacob, whose fight left him with a bum hip. This doesn't preclude the blessing but makes us aware of receiving the undeserved love of God. It makes us realize that we must struggle in life—for example, with greed, pride, impurity, or selfishness—until we are ready to accept God's transforming grace.

> *Fight the good fight of faith, seize the eternal life to which you were called when you nobly professed your faith before many witnesses. (1 Tm 6:12)*

And you

At this point in your life you know that a bed of roses is not standard issue for a follower of Christ. If you ask around, you'll find that very few folks have an easy life. The blessing comes with the effort to transform life's woes into a willingness to suffer whatever comes your way. This is the life God gave you, and he wills that you find within it your way to his Kingdom.

Age-Appropriate

Persecuted

When we buy gifts, especially for children, we aim for something winsome or age-appropriate. However, the first example of gift-giving in the New Testament seems to have been disastrous.

After a long and hard preparation, three very wise men travel a great distance and arrive at the place where Mary and Joseph are staying with their newborn. Two of them present smartly chosen, highly valued gifts: one gives gold, the other gives frankincense. Both of these gifts are useful and are omens of a happy future for the child. The third wise man, perhaps timidly, approaches with an odd and awkward gift: myrrh. Today it would be like gifting new parents with a jar of embalming fluid or a plush skull and crossbones for their precious little one. Myrrh was the symbol of suffering and death. How off the mark was this man's gift?

Actually, in historical perspective, the man was a gift-giving guru. Myrrh was very appropriate for this child, the

Son of God, who would gain our salvation through his suffering and death. These three visitors were truly wise—quite probably prophets, as evidenced by their choice of gifts. Of course, with three particular prophetic gifts, one man had to be left holding the less desirable one. Prophets do not always see, nor do they necessarily understand, the eternal significance of what they do. In this case, the wise men chose to give what was precious in their estimation, and with these in hand they stepped into history.

Prophecy will pass away, speaking in tongues will cease, knowledge will pass away. Our knowledge is incomplete and prophecy is incomplete, but when what is perfect comes the imperfect will pass away. (1 Cor 13:8–10)

And you

Although you may not put it this way, you really do live with righteousness as your goal, that is, to live in the presence of God and for his purposes. In the case of the eighth beatitude, God asks you to accept a share in persecution for his sake. Certain forms of persecution come with the territory for those trying to live by God's rules. Being a disciple of Jesus Christ involves a prophetic, other-worldly sense. Can you stand with the Lord through the thick and thin of discipleship?

55

Cunning

Persecuted

In Massachusetts we don't call our parents' sisters and sisters-in-law—our aunties—"Antie," but rather "*Ah*-ntie." I was blessed with lots of aunts, but only one great-aunt named Lottie. She and my Nana were from *down* Maine, as they put it—a geographic mystery to me. Among their many endearing expressions was *Eh-yah*, which meant anything from *yes* to *no*, *perhaps*, *what*, *you don't say*, or *true*. I think this word alone earned for Mainers their claim to being thrifty. The other word that always fascinated me was *cunning*, which they lovingly applied to babies and all their accoutrements. "The baby is so cunning in that little suit," they'd say.

We're more familiar with that word as Jesus applied it to his enemies, calling them cunning as foxes. He meant that they were sly and devious. Jesus went about announcing the Kingdom and preaching the Good News; his enemies went about trying to trip him up. Jesus wove wonderful, touching examples from the fabric of daily life. He put in great effort to make his Father's love and concern palpable to his hearers. His cunning enemies devised obtuse problems for Jesus, such as the case of the woman who married seven brothers (see Mt 22:23–33). They even penetrated Jesus' inner circle of apostles to find a traitor.

If nothing else, persecution is often persistent and always cunning. In speaking of the greatest traitor—Satan, who turned on God himself—Jesus described the devil as going about like a prowling lion, looking for someone to devour. What defense do we have against such powers? Our best defense is our effort to live the beatitudes. As we have seen in these pages, the beatitudes are the ways of holy cunning.

Beloved, don't be surprised at the fiery ordeal which has come among you to test you, as if something strange were happening; instead, rejoice insofar as you are sharing in Christ's sufferings, so that when his glory is revealed you may rejoice and exult. (1 Pt 4:12–13)

And you

Reflect on this: Poverty of spirit leaves room for God, mourning softens and shapes you to God's comfort, meekness fills you with quiet strength, yearning for righteousness gives you holy alertness, mercy makes you a mirror of the divine, purity of heart keeps your attention fixed on God, peacefulness gives you a sense of empathy for others. All of these beatitudes arm you with everything you need.

56

Minor Prophets

Persecuted

When we travel down highways, we are bombarded with billboards. Today some are actual movie screens, flashing and twirling for our attention.

On the highway between San Diego and Los Angeles, recent signage went well over the top. Years ago drivers were distracted by actual cars fastened hundreds of feet in the air, but with one, new, animated ad a car would suddenly appear racing toward you. It was a terrifying sight at night. To see glaring headlights barreling into your peripheral vision while you were concentrating on five or six lanes of traffic was very disconcerting. Hopefully this particular ad is history!

I've found in my long driving career that billboards range from cleverly amusing to downright annoying. And the world will find us the same. As prophets of the Kingdom, we will be tolerated as deluded and quaint or criticized for being strident and overbearing. But prophets we are! Because we are members of Christ, we share in his identity as priest, prophet, and king. Just thinking about our role as a prophet, we may be tempted to timidity. However, being prophetic in this case simply means being an authentic disciple of Jesus.

We ourselves, as minor prophets, need the major prophetic examples we find in the likes of Dorothy Day, Joan Andrews Bell, Mother Teresa, Oscar Romero, and Sister Dorothy Stang. We should not get sidetracked by any political overtones, but rather stare intently at the determined and heroic witness each of them tried to give to the Gospel in the here-and-now. These great folks were inspired to witness "to the extreme"; some might find them an embarrassment, but we need such demonstrations of dedication to inspire us.

Our witness is not likely to be so dramatic, but will be lived out within the boundaries of a regularly scheduled life. Our prophecy of the Kingdom of God—that is, our sincere practice of Catholicism—will hopefully be the stimulus for someone else in turn.

> *Who will separate us from Christ's love? Affliction, distress, persecution, famine, destitution, danger, or the sword? . . . But, in all these things we are winning an overwhelming victory through the One Who loved us. (Rom 8:35, 37)*

And you

Have you known individuals who inspired you to be more committed to Christ, perhaps a grandparent or a member of the parish? Do you think anyone will find in you a Catholic role model?

But What About Suffering?

Necessary Note

We do so many things, say so many prayers, make so many sacrifices, and still God lets us suffer. Why?

We could brashly say: *Why not?* But it isn't God who *makes* us suffer. Suffering is part of being human. How many people do you know who don't suffer anything?

Why can't God take suffering away from his faithful ones? The answer is simple and sublime: because God trusts us with suffering. As Christians we're part of the Mystical Body of God's Son. We're one with Christ. So when the Father looks at us, he sees Jesus—especially if we are trying to be devoted, prayerful, loving people. That means God is our all and we are intent on loving and caring for people. The Father, then, sees in us the same heart that he sees in his Son and thereby trusts us to know the meaning and merit of suffering.

Blessed Mother Teresa of Calcutta reminds us that "to resolve to be a saint costs much. Renunciations, temptations, struggles, persecutions, and all kinds of sacrifices surround the resolute soul. One can love God only at one's own expense."[1]

Jesus didn't miraculously heal a sinful world; he did it through his own humanity: living our life and dying our worst death. God trusts us because he sees Christ in us: *Will you, my son, my daughter, use your human suffering to benefit humanity?* Saint Paul said: "I rejoice in what I am suffering for you now; in my flesh I am completing what is lacking in Christ's afflictions on behalf of his body, that is, the church" (Col 1:24).

Jesus is the Son of God, so what is lacking? Our participation, our identifying with Christ; our willingness to go the whole way; our owning the act of redemption. As when we go into the inner city and help rebuild homes or refurbish schools and playgrounds—hoping that the people living there will have a spirit of ownership and that the renewal will belong to and be continued by them—so it is with the redemption and our suffering.

> . . . *Born in human likeness, and to all appearances a man.*
> *He humbled himself and became obedient,*
> *even unto death, death on a cross. (Phil 2:7–8)*

And you

None of this takes the pain out of suffering. As Christ entered our humanity, may we also enter fully into being human and reconcile with our poor, weak humanity that will be raised up with him to the act of redeeming love.

Happily Ever After

Wrap up of the beatitudes

What do we most expect of a fairy tale? Why, a happy ending, of course! At least this is what we usually hope for. And yet, we complain when certain TV dramas portray a happy ending against all odds; we say they have become contrived and saccharine. We like our dramas to reflect the drama of our own very real lives. Happiness, yes, but realistic, adjustable happiness—something constructed from the mismatched pieces of our lives.

Advertising campaigns for a "must-have" product make a lot of claims and promises. "If you buy this or commit yourself to that, you will receive the following rewards. . . ." As we have seen, Jesus makes a hard sell in the Gospel when he presents the *beatitudes*. He tries to interest us in the mega-reward of eternal happiness, but somehow we hear a rather difficult proposal.

The beatitudes spoken by Jesus inhabit both worlds—the one beneath our feet and the one beyond our imagining.

Remember this point when speaking about the Gospel beatitudes. Each beatitude has two parts; each gives a *here* and a *hereafter*. These two segments are contingent on one another. For example, the fifth beatitude says: *Blessed are the merciful, for they shall receive mercy.* It takes little imagination to realize that in our present life the merciful do not always receive mercy. How often we read of an individual who offered financial assistance to someone in need only to have his credit card account hacked by that same person. Closer to daily life, how often are smiles ignored or attempts at reconciliation rebuffed? Do these negative responses render the merciful person not blessed? Not in the least (however, it does make clearer the difference between *blessed* and *happy*). The one rebuffed is likely unhappy about it, but nevertheless blessed because of the effort.

> *This is what you were called to and this is why Christ suffered for you—to leave you an example for you to follow in his footsteps.* (1 Pt 2:21)

And you

Having spent some time reflecting on the eight beatitudes, are you clearer on their meaning for your daily living as a disciple of Christ? Do you feel more attuned to one in particular? Try thinking of the other seven in the light of that one.

THE SERMON ON THE MOUNT

CONTINUES IN MATTHEW 5:13—7:29

2B or Not 2B

The Choice

"To be or not to be" is a very serious and important consideration. In Shakespeare's *Hamlet* it was a matter of life or death. For me, as I traveled home alone from New York, it was a matter of which exit to take: 2B or another one. Here a wrong choice could lead down a lengthy hardtop path. Turnoffs and additional exits were at a premium, and rest stops were non-existent. I imagine if I were a man, never would I have even indicated a dilemma was at hand. And never would I have uttered that four-letter word: LOST.

Whatever did we do without that electronic gizmo that so sweetly announces all the twists and turns of our journey? Unfortunately, in life we all have the tendency to deviate a bit in order to glance, to gaze, or to gawk at one thing or another. Fortunately for us, soon enough our attention is drawn back to our original purpose and we hear the little voice of conscience saying: "Re-calculating, re-calculating, re-calculating. . . ." Serious deviation requires actually turning around and retracing our route. Lesser deviations can be corrected simply by taking a "right-turn-ahead" and threading our way back to the right road.

Jesus gave us this little portion of the Gospel, Matthew 5:3–12, as a tracking device. The beatitudes are intended to point out the way for us to navigate through the subtleties and inconsistencies of our journey to heaven. Immediately after this passage Jesus adds some thoughts on living the commandments, as if to offer us examples of what the beatitudes will look like in the life of the believer (see Mt 5:12–7:29).

> *"In a little while the world will no longer*
>   *see me, but you will see me;*
> *because I will live, you, too, will live.*
> *On that day you will realize that I am in my Father,*
>   *and you in me and I in you.*
> *Whoever keeps my commandments and obeys them—*
>   *he it is who loves me,*
> *While whoever loves me is loved by my Father,*
>   *and I'll love him and reveal myself to him."*
>   *(Jn 14:19–21)*

And you

In the next few chapters, see if you can identify the influence of the beatitudes. For example, how does the third beatitude assist us in living the fifth commandment? Do you find a trace of the first beatitude throughout the commandments?

"You da Man!"

After beatitudes

"What did he say?"

We were reading children's essays about gratitude. Gales of laughter greeted Sister Madonna as she shared little Johnny's declaration. "I'm glad Jesus was born," he wrote, "otherwise I'd be following the bad example of someone else."

Awesome! Johnny just gave the classic backhanded compliment. A compliment is a compliment, however! For Johnny, Jesus is the greatest.

Young people today often say to one another: "You da man!" Putting grammar aside, this is a very affirmative accolade. It conveys esteem, respect, gratitude, admiration, and a myriad of other good things.

With utmost respect each of us can look at our awesome Lord and say to him: "You da Man!" How often do we hear him addressed this way? Well, not very often, and truthfully not often enough, for if anyone is *the* Man it is Jesus. He, of all men, is the center of strength and joy, the true measure of our existence. Wouldn't it be grand if all of us—young and old and in between—would affirm *the* Man, Jesus Christ!

Jesus is the unique man because he is Son of God and born of a Virgin. He became one of us as a man to redeem us from the horrible weight of sin brought upon us by the first man's sin of disobedience. Jesus is our Way, Truth, and Life, as he describes himself (see Jn 14:6). He is the true man, the man of truth, the exemplar of what it means to be a man, and the giver of love and the grace we need to live as children of God. He is *man par excellence.*

In the beatitudes Jesus offered a résumé of discipleship. He said: *In these statements of blessing I am describing not just myself, but each of my disciples.* And we thank you, Jesus, because "you da Man."

> *"You have heard that it was said to the ancients. . . . But I say to you. . . ." (Mt 5:21–22)*

And you

Who has more right to tell us what the Father wants of us than Jesus? He came as our Teacher and is our Redeemer. Is Jesus also the Man in your life? How devoted to him are you? Is his word your guide and joy?

The Saline Solution

Salt of the Earth

MATTHEW 5:13

Most people will concede that today we have an obsession with salt. We can hardly think of cooking without it (it makes water boil faster, we say). We sprinkle salt on so many things that we eat (to bring out the taste, we say). But sometimes we can have too much of a good thing. By over-salting our diet we are, in fact, killing ourselves.

In Jesus' time, when Mary was in the kitchen, salt was still a luxury. People used it judiciously. This was why Jesus told his followers that they would be a saline solution for the world's problems. Life in their world had gone flat. In a sense folks were playing it safe since Rome had taken over. Yes, occasional uprisings broke out, but by and large people had a live-and-let-live attitude. *We live our way and the Romans live their way, but we won't raise any dust. Don't draw attention to the differences, but blend into the scene that's been set.*

That is why Jesus of Nazareth became a crisis point in Jerusalem. His novel preaching energized and excited people so much that lots of them followed him wherever he went. This took them away from their normal occupations; they were abandoning the norm to attend what today might appear to be rallies. The Romans seemed content only to observe this daring young rabbi. Some of the Jewish authorities, however, were looking for ways to get him out of the spotlight. They were so focused on maintaining a truce with the Romans that they didn't notice the plan God had afoot. God sent this young man, his own Son, to begin a reform—not just of Israel, but of the whole world. Jerusalem was center stage, the beginning of something entirely new.

And to his disciples Jesus said: "You are the salt of the earth," the central actors, the difference makers.

"But if the salt should lose its taste,
what can it be salted with?
It's good for nothing but to be thrown outside
and be trampled underfoot." (Mt 5:13)

And you

As a follower of Christ today you are this salt for the world. How do you try to enhance the flavor of things around you in a Christian way?

Weathering Heights

Light of the world

MATTHEW 5:14–16

You thought of Emily Brontë's book, didn't you? *Wuthering Heights* is a masterpiece of nineteenth-century literature set on England's windswept moors. But I'm thinking of our collective trek over the wild *mores* of our twenty-first century lives. Brontë's heroine was trapped in a loveless existence of her own choice, surrounded by the bleak but wildly compelling landscape. The particulars of our existence can be set anywhere, on any horizon, as we face our spiritual struggles. Hence the heights! And hence the weathering of heights!

The spiritual life—that is, our trek toward the Kingdom of God—is an upward journey. And sometimes we can just about make it from one step to the next because we are working our way to heaven while working our way through our earthly life. In this life the weather is always changing through the various seasons: some warm and beautiful, others wild and wind-blown. Weathering the heights of holiness is definitely challenging. The good news is that God's Kingdom, which is atop the heights of holiness, is a very well-lit city and we, who were given our citizenship there by our baptism, carry the city's light within us. This wondrous light is called grace. We don't see it, but we do see by it.

Jesus declares us "light of the world." Neither the city nor we the citizens can be hidden because we are "set atop a mountain." By keeping our own light shining as we travel the heights, we are lighting the way for fellow travelers. We know from experience that keeping the light on is a welcoming thing. In very practical terms, it means that by living as committed and convinced Christians we are a welcoming light to others.

> *"Let your light so shine before men*
> *that they will see your good works*
> *and glorify your Father in Heaven." (Mt 5:16)*

And you

When we set out for a climb, we wisely prepare our supplies ahead of time. If we may encounter darkness or stormy weather, we bring a lamp. And we make sure our companions are similarly set for the trek.

Our moors are the particulars of our moral life, and it's a climb you cannot decide against. Do you take extra care that your inner light is strong and steady to guide your steps and those of others?

Up the Ante

Righteousness

MATTHEW 5:17–20

Anything you can do, I can do better. When I was in training to become a religious sister, I began a playful verbal competition with one of my companions. At recreation we would constantly intone the challenge: "Anything you can do, I can do better. I can do anything better than you." Well, in the long run my companion won. Over the years she has proved more capable in any number of fields. Yet, even though just two of us were competing, I don't exactly feel like the loser because I came in a very satisfying second.

We do find Jesus "upping the ante" for all of his disciples. He calls us to a better way even when it comes to the practice of God's law. Some folks seem to think that the New Law is all that matters and they disregard some of the commandments, for example. Others appear to zero in on the severity of the Old Law as the way to go and forget Jesus' stress on mercy. However, Jesus speaks very clearly to all of us: "Don't think that I came to overturn the Torah or the Prophets; I came not to destroy but to fulfill." According to Jesus, not even the tiniest stroke of a letter in the Law is to be eliminated. Nothing is to be modified or abbreviated. To do this is to buy a ticket to the cheap seats in the Kingdom. For Jesus, there is a big difference between abolishing the Law and fulfilling it, that is, bringing it to perfection.

Jesus also says something surprising about those who are dedicated to living God's law. He says: "Unless your righteousness greatly exceeds that of the scribes and Pharisees, you'll never enter into the Kingdom of Heaven." What does he mean by this? Perhaps Jesus is saying that these lawyers and teachers were holy, but not in a life-giving way. They were stifling their own spirit and that of the people. Their holiness was only external, to be admired. In a sense, they were concentrating solely on looking holy and observant.

> *"But whoever obeys and teaches the commandments,*
>> *he shall be called great in the Kingdom of Heaven."*
>> *(Mt 5:19)*

And you

Jesus came to "up the ante." Less than best won't do. All he wants to hear is that you are "all in." How into his teaching are you?

Packing Heat

Anger

MATTHEW 5:21–26

If you are like me, you're overwhelmed by the number of murders reported in the news—the *daily* news! It's as if our society is reverting to lawlessness. True, most killers are caught, but they seem unconcerned about that ahead of time.

Murder is a sin that seems far from my life, but anger is an all too familiar failing. Jesus puts anger squarely at the root of murder. He even warns against using abusive language. I'm afraid that if we took him seriously on this point we would be attending silent movies on many a Saturday night (not to mention what would happen with certain genres of song lyrics, TV shows, and even common conversations).

Why do we use abusive language? It seems to come from an angry spirit or, if you prefer, an angered spirit. Jesus spells out for us the almost inevitable route from anger to contempt to murder. By coddling our anger we are actually packing heat, so to speak. But, as our soul's Divine Physician, Jesus is also offering us the cure for this smoldering flame we take for granted.

Jesus is presuming that although we admit to possessing a short fuse, we are still practicing Christians. He offers this curative: "So if you're presenting your offering at the altar and remember there that your brother has something against you [or you against him], leave your offering there before the altar and first go be reconciled with your brother, and then you can come and make your offering" (Mt 5:23–24). Our life of worship is our salvation. This makes perfect sense because God wants us pure of heart, free of anger and wrath, meek and humble of heart before we present ourselves for his blessing.

"Anyone who is angry with his brother
shall be liable to judgment,
and whoever says to his brother, 'Raqa!'
shall be liable to the Sanhedrin,
and whoever says, 'You fool!'
shall be liable to the fire of Gehenna." (Mt 5:22)

And you

We shouldn't look for Jesus' cure only when presenting ourselves before the altar for Mass, but also whenever we pray—for example, morning or evening prayer. Do you include a little look at your actions and emotions when you glance over your day? Do you humbly acknowledge your failings and resolve to try again?

From This Day Froth

Adultery

MATTHEW 5:27–32

I had just squished myself between passengers on the train when a sullen-looking young woman asked if I was a nun. "Yes," I replied.

"How long you been?"

"Forty-six years," I said.

Stunned she said, "You must have a lot of self-control."

I had no comeback other than a profound, "Hmm, I guess." What I really guess is that this isn't a concept that occurs to those of us living a religious vocation. I pronounced my vows many years back, and, thanks be to God, I've no desire to go back on my word. I do realize, however, that self-control can be a struggle for some folks.

At this point in the Sermon on the Mount Jesus seems to be making it even harder for us to, well, "have a lot of self-control." He says to the people: although you have been taught not to commit adultery, I'm saying that you shouldn't even look at anyone with lustful thoughts. One might think: Doesn't he understand how human nature works? Indeed he does, and he is giving us some sage advice. He is telling us we will have fewer falls from grace in this area if we keep track of our thoughts. If we allow the mind and heart free rein, soon enough the body will demand the same freedom. If we remain faithful to virtue, we will remain faithful to the commitments of our vocation.

In her delightful verse, "Lake of Beer," Saint Brigid of Ireland notes that "the happy heart is true." The pure of heart have a joyful view of their commitments. When we look at a beer mug, the froth is only a sign of the possibility of pleasure, but the rich reward is in the taste. We need to keep the known joy of the taste we have freely chosen and not let our attention stray to the froth on another brand. Likewise, when thinking of our present commitment, we can decide that from this day forward everything else, no matter how attractive and available, is froth.

> *"I say to you that anyone who looks at a woman with lust for her has already committed adultery with her in his heart."*
> *(Mt 5:28)*

And you

How do your treat your life commitment? If you are married, do you spend your energy on this shared blessing with your spouse? Do you view distractions as mere froth, to be blown away in favor of the substance?

Sense and Sensibility

Swearing

MATTHEW 5:33–42

Most of the time when we swear an oath, we use a lot of extra words to verbalize what should just be an exclamation point. Our oath says something like this: *"I'm really serious here!"* or *"You'd better believe me: how's this over-the-top statement to prove my point?"* Of course, we do make some serious oaths, for example: "I swear to tell the truth, the whole truth, and nothing but the truth, so help me God." However, in the verses cited above we hear Jesus telling us not to utter any oaths, not to swear at all. Why not, since everyone does for emphasis? Jesus' reason is so sensible. He tells us that we should be so reliable that it would never cross anyone else's mind to doubt the truth of what we say. Our daily dealings with others, whether friendly or in serious or unsettling situations, should always be upright. Why should we feel a need to cover our verbal tracks? If you are an honest, trustworthy person, all swearing is wasted breath.

It's far better to save our hot breath to warm our hands on cold mornings and not to blow smoke screens over mental missteps. In the Old Law it was said that one should not swear falsely, but carry out all that one solemnly promises. Jesus goes a step beyond and declares there should be no swearing of oaths at all. Why? So we don't call on God to witness our weakness. Neither heaven nor earth nor God's throne should be brought in to witness what we alone are responsible for, which only we who have sworn can carry out. It's also useless to swear on our own head (or on our mother's grave); as the Lord reminds us, we can't make even one hair white or black (at least not by merely willing it). When we say "yes" or "no," mean it, he says. Every other word spoken on a promise is fluff or bluff and very likely from the devil.

"Let your 'yes,' be 'yes,' and your 'no,' 'no'; anything more than that is from the Evil One." (Mt 5:37)

And you

Not only does Jesus teach us to avoid swearing and making oaths to bolster what should be our natural truthfulness, our personal sensibility also guides us. Think of what your spirit whispers to you when you are tempted to tamper with the truth.

Dreaded Dust Bunnies

Love of neighbors

MATTHEW 5:43–48

In the piddling glow of a two-watt nightlight, I saw it. It was bigger than I wanted to face alone. *Oh, it's also furry, and I'm sure I saw it move. Can I jump out of bed and switch on the ceiling light before it notices me?* Success! But in the blazing light from above, I saw it for what it was: a dreaded dust bunny. Mother was right: a little attention to weekly dusting would have eliminated this dark phantom.

We live in paranoid days, it's true. Whether we admit it or not, we face bigger fears these days than dreaded dust bunnies. Those really are our own responsibility, but they aptly represent our reaction to the unknown. Some folks afoot in our world are truly fearsome. We can do something akin to dusting, however, to clear the scene somewhat. Jesus words this solution clearly: "You've heard that it was said, Love your neighbor! And hate your enemy. But *I* say to you, Love your enemies, and pray for those who persecute you." This may seem an impossible proposition, because our natural inclination is to protect at least our common sense. But as Christians this *is* our common sense: to act just as Jesus did. He never attacked those who were against him. In fact, in his passion he could have obliterated his enemies, but he didn't. What will we use as our excuse for acting contrary to our Lord? Jesus tells us that this is the same crazy love that God the Father has for the good and the bad. We can't simply love, care, respect, and converse with those who are like us. Jesus asks, "What great thing are you doing?" No, as followers of the Prince of Peace we must strive to be perfect as the heavenly Father is perfect. Possible? Not literally, but in intention and by our effort to mirror the Son, the Father will recognize us as his own reflection.

> *"He causes his sun to rise on the evil and the good,*
> *and rain to fall on the just and the unjust." (Mt 5:45)*

And you

Realistically speaking, you and I know there are enemies of everyone and everything we hold sacred and valuable. Can you hold these enemies up to the Father in prayer? By keeping the light of love in your heart, you risk sharing in divine perfection.

Golden Eggs

Purity of intention

MATTHEW 6:1–4

A charming Italian dismissive goes like this: *Don't pretend to be the daughter of the white chicken.* In other words, stop acting as if you're special. My guess is that in some parts of Italy most chickens have darker feathers, and a white one is set apart and pampered (however you do that for a fowl).

Sometimes we are tempted to look at our virtues as if they were quite unusual. Here is a word of warning from the great Lutheran theologian, Dietrich Bonhoeffer: "Who is pure in heart? Only those who have surrendered their hearts completely to Jesus that he may reign in them alone. Only those whose hearts are undefiled by their own evil—and by their own virtues too."[1]

Sometimes, to use another poultry-related analogy, we treat our "goodness" like the golden egg in Aesop's fables. Because the farmers thought the hen laying a daily golden orb must be solid gold inside, they killed her. Sadly, she was no different on the inside than any other chick. In regard to our own goodness, purity of intention is very difficult to maintain, precisely because by nature we are so drawn to recognition and a reputation like one of the "golden ones." However, too much admiration and examination can insidiously dry up such lustrous virtue.

Jesus says that when we do something good we should keep it secret even from ourselves, if that were possible. In other words, do it and then let it go. No admiring the golden egg. God is in charge of the reward because, after all, he gave us the ability to conceive the good idea, the will to carry it out, and the strength to actually do it.

"Take care not to perform your good deeds in front of others in order to be seen by them, if you do, you will have no reward from your Father in Heaven." (Mt 6:1)

And you

Acting with purity of intention is a bit difficult, because we have a hard time distinguishing our good works from our very self. (Too bad we don't lay such a strong claim on our mistakes!) Do you give what is golden in you *without letting your left hand know what your right hand is doing*?

The Stick Figure

Prayerfulness

MATTHEW 6:5–6

Saint Simeon the Stylite was one interesting man. He lived for forty years atop a platform elevated from the ground on a pillar. Hence, his title: the Stylite, or the person on the pole or stick. This was admirable piety, and for his time a great witness to prayer and penance. His example, however, doesn't do much for us moderns because we can imagine a rather bad scene after being aloft for that long. Nonetheless, Simeon's stance made an obvious statement.

Although Jesus warned his followers against praying in a manner to be seen, Simeon was making a statement on the need to pray. He had tried a monastery, but was turned away. He attempted to hole himself up in solitude as a hermit, but people sought him out because of his holiness. In fact, Simeon also made several attempts on pillars of various heights before discovering his final perch, which was a couple of stories high. Certain disciples brought him food and drink, and some who sought his advice were allowed to come up to him by a ladder. So up there on his rather small platform Simeon spent his days in prayer and acts of penance. Certainly it was an extreme witness to the necessity of prayer, but he *did* inspire others to take their prayer life more seriously.

We are not called to do anything as dramatic as Saint Simeon. Neither backyard tree houses nor parish choir lofts can make Stylites of us. Our prayer is to be more normal, in fact, most normal. Jesus says: "Go into your storeroom and shut the door" when you pray. In other words, pray from within your life as it is. Pray naturally from your heart about your life, your needs, your desires. Shut out all the temptations to showiness, whether in practice or in posture. One of the most common follies of the truly prayerful is to sneak glimpses of themselves at prayer. God does the looking, and he sees what is hidden in our hearts.

> *"Pray to your Father who is hidden,*
> *and your Father who sees what is hidden will*
> *reward you." (Mt 6:6)*

And you

What form of prayer seems to be "your storeroom," where you find the comfort and strength to live as a true disciple of Christ? Are you able to enter into your prayer easily, putting aside unnecessary distractions?

Scribbles

Prayerfulness

MATTHEW 6:7–15

The most remarkable finds made when the city of Pompeii was unearthed included the graffiti on the sides of buildings. It seems that these outer walls were commonly used as bulletin boards. Lots of political campaign notices were found, as well as announcements for gladiatorial games, advertisements for rentals, and honest-to-goodness graffiti: *Marcus was here!* or *Julius loves Claudia!* All this writing inspired someone to scribble this verse: *I'm amazed you don't collapse, O walls, beneath the weight of all these scrawls!*

If we had to post all our prayers on a wall, I suppose the space would soon be taken up with all of our petitions, intercessions, confessions, and words of praise. Luckily for us, God hears and remembers our prayers.

Lots of words aren't even needed. God isn't impressed by the quantity or quality of words; he is moved by sincerity. We wonder then: If he already knows what we'll ask as well as what we need, why do we pray at all? In his wisdom God knows that not only do we need to express our prayers to him, but we also need to hear ourselves say them. By hearing and expressing our prayerfulness consciously, we are more engaged. While formulation isn't necessary for God to receive our prayer, placing words to prayer makes it a more normal human action. It makes us feel more at home with prayer when it becomes conversation.

As man Jesus also prayed, and he shared one prayer as a model for us. In the *Lord's Prayer* we too praise the name of God as Father, we ask that his Kingdom come as he promised, that his will be done here on earth as it's done in heaven. We pray to be sustained by daily bread, to be forgiven as we forgive, to be spared temptation, and to be rescued from all evil. We seal this with an "amen," the prayerful equivalent of a firm handshake or a tender kiss.

> *"For your Father knows what you need before you ask him." (Mt 6:8)*

And you

Jesus tacked a not-so-little catch after the *Our Father*. He says that for our offenses to be forgiven, we have to be willing to forgive whatever comes our way. If we refuse to at least try, we won't be forgiven by God. I'd say this is something worth working at. How about you?

Look the Part

Looking prayerful

MATTHEW 6:16–18

Everyone likes "to put one over." Not only do we delight in being pranksters, but we love pulling off the big surprise, like the military parent who pretends to be the pizza delivery person or the mascot at a ball park—and then comes the happy revealing!

Great actors and actresses have the uncanny ability to assume the appearance and personality of their characters. It is amazing how they can cause us to suspend our belief: are we actually looking at Queen Elizabeth or Abraham Lincoln on the screen? This is a true art form.

Jesus gives us directions on how to appear when we pray. As a matter of fact, he dedicated some time to those who seek recognition from others when they pray. He chided the Pharisees for assuming obvious prayer postures while standing out on street corners; for widening their phylacteries (the equivalent of the sacred objects we wear) so others could better admire their piety, and enlarging the tassels worn at the ends of their prayer shawls to make them more noticeable (see Mt 23:5). Sometimes we have trouble distinguishing the line between ostentation and witness, but a helpful practice is to always check our motivations: Is this for God or for me?

Jesus now directs our attention to one of the triplets of piety, which are prayer, fasting, and almsgiving. His advice regarding fasting reminds me of something a retired nursing friend shared. Along with all the basic nursing skills, her instructor insisted that the student nurses never go on duty without carefully applying their makeup. "Your patients deserve to see you at your best," she would say. "They are already not feeling well, so besides the care you provide, you need to lift their spirits by looking your best."

In a sense, this is Jesus' advice to us when we decide to fast. As with all acts of mortification and penance, they are best left between God and us. Otherwise, merit is easily lost and pride is easily gained. Jesus suggests one surefire way to hide these sacrifices: avoid looking the part.

> "But when you fast, anoint your head
>   and wash your face,
>   so others won't see that you are fasting." (Mt 6:17–18)

And you

Do you have a strategy at work or school for fasting (and abstaining in Lent) without being too obvious? What other things besides food can you fast from?

72

Fringe Benefits

Treasure

MATTHEW 6:19–23

Not long ago while on a trip, I realized that my coffee-shop gift card was missing. After rifling through my suitcase, handbag, and pockets—then my room, the rest of the house, and the car—I settled into a mild state of panic. While mentally retracing my steps, I remembered that at the airport I had emptied my pockets into a metal detector basket. Did I retrieve it? Or, of course, the card could have fallen from my pocket on the plane—the seats are tight and after a few hours, feeling is all but lost in some extremities. Goodness, anything could have happened. In an airport as large as the one I'd just landed at, there could have been a pickpocket in need of a simple cup of joe. But where had my coffee card gone? Finally, I asked my companion if she had noticed what I'd done with it, but she hadn't. I worried and fretted endlessly about that blessed gift card. The good Lord smiled down, reminding me of what I was really losing: "Don't store up treasures for your-selves on earth, where moth and rust destroy, where thieves break in and steal." "Now, besides a coffee card," he continued, "you are in danger of losing your love for me." Well, that would never do, would it? So I filed my missing gift card report in the back of my mind and returned to being an attentive disciple of Christ.

Certainly many things in life do deserve our attention, and at times these concerns seem to distract us from the path of Christian perfection. Jesus likens this need for attention to how we use our eyes. Used "generously," he says, our eyes will provide light for the entire human edifice, but if we are "grudging" with the gift of sight, darkness will be the measure of the day. So the remedy is to keep the light of Christ always before us, so every step of the day will lead to the real treasure.

"For where your treasure is,
there will your heart be too." (Mt 6:21)

And you

Did I mention that my gift card miraculously reappeared in a pocket that I thought I had checked? Do you ever find yourself undone by things: lost, desired, stolen, denied, misplaced, or even needed? Can you redirect your heart to your one true treasure?

73

Betwixt and Between

Reliance

MATTHEW 6:24–34

Do you suffer from the "rock and hard place" syndrome? You're probably so busy negotiating these straits that you don't have time to even name the problem. Jesus warns us of the danger of trying to serve two masters. You'll end up preferring one and trying to avoid the other. A classic example of this would be the man or woman who tries to maintain two relationships. The love and devotion owed to the one is stolen to please the other, and disaster awaits if the deceit is discovered. Jesus says we can't serve God and mammon, that is, we need to choose between the ruler of this world and the ruler of the next. *Well,* you might think, *why must we choose? Can't we just give due attention to each?* Consider another example. An Austrian farmer, husband, and father, Franz Jägerstätter was inducted into the army of the Third Reich. He had hoped to elude the moment before him, but the army—desperate for manpower—was calling up everyone. Franz offered to act as a medic, but was denied. Finally, he boldly stated, "I cannot serve. In fact, I can't even wear the uniform of such an evil regime." Needless to say, he was thrown into prison. No amount of pleading or cajoling by relatives, friends, or even his pastor could get Franz to compromise for the sake of his family. "Only my wife understands what my resolve means," he sorrowfully said, "and I apologize to her for this pain." Having lived his youth in wild recklessness, Franz deeply appreciated the faith and commitment that now encompassed him. Rather than compromise, he willingly faced the wrath of the Nazi machine. "From my own experience," he stated, "I can attest how painful life can be when one lives Christianity only halfway. It is vegetating, not living." On August 9, 1943, Franz's choice for God was sealed with his execution.

"So don't go worrying about tomorrow—tomorrow will worry for itself. One day's evil is enough for a day." (Mt 6:34)

And you

Thinking of all your worries about this life, do you envy the lovely birds that seem to have no cares or concerns? As he does for all of nature, God provides for each of us. Can you enter into that natural climate of trust? At least do you entrust all your concerns into God's safekeeping?

74

The Inner Court

Judging

MATTHEW 7:1–5

Although I particularly hate jury duty, I have some kind of second calling to be impaneled. So many times when I've been summoned, I've also been selected and seated. Once when I tried to get myself excused as unsuitable for service, the good judge took one look at my questionnaire and declared me exactly the sort of juror they were looking for. *This isn't justice,* I thought. *I realize how valuable our court system is, but any other time I wanted to be chosen for something, it didn't happen. So why now?*

The cases I've served on have generally been interesting enough, as far as the storyline goes. I was often disappointed, however, because so much depends on how lawyers argue the case, how transparent those involved can bring themselves to be, and what actually is to be decided. Several times I wanted a different outcome from what I myself had voted for, but given the evidence and argument, the law allowed for no other possibility.

You'd think such experiences would swear me off any judging, but not so. The tendency to judge others is very strong, especially when the stakes don't seem very high. In reality, the stakes are indeed high. When we pass judgment, we do not realize the precarious position we step into. For every speck in another's eye, a beam's worth of dust clouds our own line of vision. It is all too easy to want to help another overcome a problem, but so difficult to even see one's own failings. When we set ourselves up as lawyer, witness, and judge of another, the chance of justice is quite limited. Jesus promises one thing: we will be judged with the same judgment we mete out to others.

"For God didn't send his Son into the world
to judge the world,
But to save the world through him." (Jn 3:17)

And you

Do you find yourself holding an inner court, passing judgment on the actions and intentions of others?

Hunters and Gatherers

Confidence

MATTHEW 7:6–12

Our earliest human ancestors had it tough. Of course, they had nothing to compare their conditions with. We are told that they started out as hunters who traveled with animal herds that provided for all their needs. But at some point they must have paused long enough to notice how birds inadvertently planted seeds. As these folks saw how a cycle of sun and rain caused the yield to appear, it was an "aha" moment for our whole race. The next logical step was to settle and try their hand at farming, and then gather in the crops.

Perhaps Jesus is referring to the process of hunting and gathering when he talks about asking, seeking, and knocking. God the Father is the Gatherer who continues to send out the invitation because he is eager to give. And we, the Hunters, are all about asking. We just aren't always as persistent as God hopes we'll be, nor do we always recognize an answer even when it is staring us in the face. However, we learn from God to give appropriately, as Jesus says: not things of the spirit to dogs, or human riches to swine. They can't appreciate these gifts and may take them wrongly and attack us. To impress upon us the goodness of God's gifts, Jesus reminds us that we too know what to give our children—never anything that would hurt or disappoint them. So, if even we, who are weak-willed and often slow to comprehend because of the sinfulness of our nature, willingly give only good to our kids, how much more will God our Father in heaven give good to those who ask him?

> "Therefore, whatever you want others to do for you,
>   do so for them as well;
> For this is the Torah and the Prophets." (Mt 7:12)

And you

Do you ever question God's good gifts when they seem slow in coming or when something harmful or hurtful does come your way? Speak with God about this with humble faith and childlike confidence.

Take some time to look at how you respond to the requests others make of you. Are you able to "hear" even what is unspoken?

The Squeeze

Narrow Way

MATTHEW 7:13–20

As a diversion one fine summer day we went to see the sights in New Hampshire. At this time the noble Old Man in the Mountain, the very symbol of the Granite State, was still overlooking the area. We visited the stunning Flume Gorge and then made our way to the Polar Caves, very cold and very narrow in places. To give an idea of how narrow, note the name given to one section: the Lemon Squeeze. The "fun" here involves squirming over very tight boulder formations left within the caves by ancient glaciers. I searched for a plus-sized route but didn't find one, so I was forced to use the humiliating outer Chicken Walk.

In our spiritual life we don't look for an easy way out but follow Jesus, who directs his disciples to head for the narrow gate. The only other alternative isn't pretty: the way to destruction. According to Jesus this other way is also over-crowded, while the narrow way is found by very few. If this is the case—and why would we doubt Jesus of all people—then we should be looking around for our fellow travelers, hoping to direct them to the narrow road.

Jesus also cautions us to be discerning about the concession stands we frequent along the way. Never buy from the wolf in sheep's clothing, for example. Take care when tempted to pick fruit as well. Remember you won't find grapes on thorn bushes or figs on thistles. Bring only the good fruits of the Spirit, the substantial nourishment of the faith.

> May only bliss and loving kindness
> be with me all the days of my life,
> and may I dwell in the house of the LORD for long days
> to come. (Ps 23:6)

And you

You are already on the road to eternal life. To arrive at the Father's house it is necessary to stay close to Jesus and listen carefully to his instructions. Do you keep the route Jesus indicated always before you? As you head for the narrow way, are you open to accepting the help of others and, in turn, courageous enough to invite others to journey the same route?

John the Who?

Listening

MATTHEW 7:21–27

When the Sacrament of Confirmation is to be received, many people look for religious articles in our stores. Often they ask about a particular saint. Once a woman came in and asked to see a statue of Saint John. "Are you thinking of John the Baptist or John the Evangelist?" Sister asked. "Oh, neither of them," the woman quickly replied. "I want John the Catholic!"

The titles of these two great saints may be easily confused, but both men were exactly what Jesus had in mind when he called followers to himself. There should never be any question about who we are either. Even if we don't say a single word, others will know by our demeanor, attitudes, and reactions, by our care and concern, that we are Christ. Yes, Christ alive among them, here and now. This is what Saint Paul prophesied about the following of Christ: "It is no longer I who live, it is Christ who lives in me!" (Gal 2:20).

Just calling out "Lord, Lord!" doesn't cut it. Doing the will of his Father is the only road to the Kingdom, and that will is to let Christ live in us.

We always grieve to hear of people in less developed parts of the world whose homes are swept away by storms and floods. "If only they could build stronger, more secure structures," we lament. This is exactly Jesus' lament as he draws his great sermon to a close. All that buffets our daily lives and our attempts to be virtuous are like the wind, rain, and floods that beat against the faithful living out of our commitment as Christians. The safeguard is so simple that we often read right through it, missing Jesus' point entirely. He says that in order not to have built our whole Christian life on sand that shifts and sinks, we need only "hear" his words and "act on them."

> "Therefore, everyone who hears these words of mine and
>   acts on them
> is like a wise man who built his house on rock." (Mt 7:24)

And you

What is there about your life that raises the suspicion that you are a Christian? Reflect on times when your words, attitudes, or gestures have let Christ into someone's life.

Heavy-Duty Concentrate

Wrap up

What is it about distraction that causes such . . . *distraction*?

One pleasant afternoon I decided to start the dishwasher. I'd done this many times before, so all should be well, right? After lining up the dishes, cups, and glasses, and putting the silverware in the proper slots, I flipped open the little door and scooped in the soap. With a flick of the wrist I closed the door, turned the dial, and pushed "Start." When I returned ten minutes later I found a billowing cloud of suds attempting to take over the entire room. I exclaimed something short of a prayer. All the steps of preparing the machine flashed before my mind, but what had I done wrong? First I turned the washer off and collected all the errant suds, which I stuffed down the sink. When I checked all the components of my near-disaster, I found that my powdered soap was labeled "Heavy-duty Concentrate"—suggested for use on witches' cauldrons, tire rims from 16-wheelers, and oatmeal kettles. So I marked one up for distraction.

As we've seen, the beatitudes speak of heavy-duty happiness. They concentrate on our likeness to Christ. It's not that the practice of the beatitudes will render *too much* happiness. Happiness will come to us as we need it, not as a momentary pause, but as an enduring, penetrating wave. So how do we explain the sufferings that continue to invade our lives? It is simply because while we're in this earthly life, our happiness—our beatitude—can still increase and expand and grow. How does this happen? Jesus tells us: it happens when you are poor in spirit; when you mourn, are meek, hunger and thirst for justice; when you are merciful, pure of heart, or make peace; and when you suffer persecution for righteousness. Our connection to the Kingdom is enhanced when we knowingly, deliberately, and lovingly live the beatitudes as Jesus spelled them out.

> *Blessed be the God and Father of our Lord Jesus Christ who has blessed us in Christ with every spiritual blessing in the heavens. He chose us in Christ before the foundation of the world to be holy and blameless before him. (Eph 1:3–4)*

And you

Do you see in the eight beatitudes a unified portrait of Christ? Looking at your life of discipleship, do you also see Christ living in you?

Happy Feat

Ending

Do you ever refer to yourself in terms used for nature—such as *making waves, having a sunny disposition,* or *bearing good fruit*? Regarding this last one, do you ever feel like a prune on a plum assignment? The first enthusiasm of following Christ—that zest for life—has dried up a bit. Our spirit, however, is the one "part" of us that should never get old and tired. The presence of God is right there within us by his ever new and life-giving grace.

What are these fruits of our spirit that should always be fresh and vibrant? We first encountered them in religion class. They're called the fruits of the Holy Spirit, who helps them flourish in us: charity, long-suffering, joy, humility, peace, faithfulness, patience, modesty, kindness, self-control, goodness, and chastity (see Gal 5:22ff.). Great-sounding stuff! The fruits are ours for the pursuing.

On reflection we can all see where these would be real assets. Possessing even a portion of this blessedness would certainly be a happy feat. Saint Thomas Aquinas says that *just as we hope for fruit when we see flowers, so we expect happiness and eternal life from virtues. As a flower is the start of a fruit, so in works of virtue is seen a beginning of everlasting blessedness.*[1]

> *"Just as the branch cannot bear fruit on its own*
> > *unless it remains on the vine,*
> *likewise you cannot unless you abide in me.*
> *I am the vine, you are the branches.*
> *Whoever abides in me, and I in him,*
> *he it is who bears much fruit,*
> *for apart from me you can do nothing. . . .*
> *If you abide in me, and my words abide in you,*
> *ask whatever you wish and it will happen for you.*
> *In this is my Father glorified,*
> *that you bear much fruit and become my disciples."*
> > *(Jn 15:4–5, 7–8)*

And you

The fruits of the Holy Spirit are the spiritual equivalent of all we do to enhance our physical appearance. They are the coloring, the liner, the powder, the blush, the close shave, the muscle milk, the aftershave, the skin cream of the soul. Do you believe that your inner beauty is reflected on your face, so that others can at least catch a glimpse of blessedness when they encounter you?

Pin the Tail on the Donkey

Kingdom

How often have you played this game at parties? A picture of a donkey is taped to a wall; you're handed a paper tail, blindfolded, spun around, and cheered on as you search for the right spot to attach your pin. Only one spot is correct. Hitting it is the game's climax, unless you play another round. The thing about life is this: we have only one round to play. It either all comes together at the right spot or not. This illustrates the importance of the beatitudes in our life. They are seen in our human activity and attitude, and that's how they define us as loving Christians. The list of beatitudes needs to be illustrated by our lives. Unless they can be "pinned on us," so to speak, they don't exist. And if the beatitudes don't inform our Christian attitude, we will be at a loss when called to the final accounting. The twenty-fifth chapter of Matthew's Gospel gives us a vivid picture of what Jesus expects of his disciples. He returns to the sheepfold motif, stating that the good folks and the bad folks will be separated as a shepherd separates sheep from goats. How this will take place depends on a little dialogue Jesus will have with each of us. He will laud us for living out the beatitudes and being a blessing to others. "When I was hungry or thirsty, a stranger, naked, sick, or in prison you cared for me," he'll say. We will ask when we saw him in these situations and looked after him. And Jesus will answer: "When you did it for one of my least ones, you in fact served me." Similarly those who find themselves condemned by Jesus will ask, "When did we neglect you, Lord?" And he will reply, "When you turned your back on those in need, you in fact turned away from me."

*"And these will go off to eternal punishment,
    but the righteous to eternal life." (Mt 25:46)*

And you

Even though in the game of life we are sometimes blindfolded, spun around, and still expected to be right on target, the effort we put forth creates the win. This is what Jesus will look for in our final résumé: Did you really try? Did you give it your all? Did you trust God's game plan and his freely given grace?

Notes

The Beatitudes

1. Blessed James Alberione, *Brevi meditazioni per ogni giorno dell'anno* [Brief Meditations for Every Day of the Year] (Rome, 1952), 162.

Chapter 7

1. Jessica Powers, *The Selected Poetry of Jessica Powers*, eds. Regina Siegfried and Robert Morneau (Washington, D.C.: ICS Publications, 1999), 55.

Chapter 18

1. Gertrude von Le Fort, *Hymns to the Church,* trans. Margaret Chanler (New York: Sheed & Ward, 1942), 44.

Chapter 19

1. J. Brian Bransfield, *Living the Beatitudes: A Journey to Life in Christ* (Boston: Pauline Books & Media, 2011), 173.

Chapter 28

1. S. Joseph Krempa, *Captured Fire: Seasonal and Sanctoral Cycle, Year Two* (Staten Island, NY: St. Pauls, 2009), 37.

Chapter 32

1. Caryll Houselander, *The Passion of the Infant Christ* (London: Sheed & Ward, 1949), 99–100.

Chapter 38

1. Simon Tugwell, *Beatitudes: Soundings in Christian Tradition* (Springfield, IL: Templegate Publishers, 1985), 90.

Chapter 46

1. Dietrich Bonhoeffer, from his English paper on "The Church and the Peoples of the World," given at the Fano Ecumenical Conference of "Life and Work," Denmark, on August 28, 1934.

Chapter 49

1. Henry Wadsworth Longfellow, *Outre-Mer and Drift-Wood* (Boston and New York: Houghton, Mifflin and Company, 1886), 405.

Chapter 57

1. Blessed Mother Teresa, *Jesus: The Word to Be Spoken: Prayers and Meditations for Every Day of the Year*, compil. Brother Angelo Devananda (New York: Walker and Company, 1987), 46.

Chapter 68

1. Dietrich Bonhoeffer, translated from the German *Nachfolge* and published in Munich by Chr. Kaiser Verlag in 1937.

Chapter 79

1. See 1a. 2ae. Q.70, a. 1